Praise for

Ten Days Without

"A fascinating read, a strong challenge, and a brilliant way to put your faith in action."

— MIKE YANKOSKI, author of *Under the Overpass*

"*Ten Days Without* is a manifesto for intentional Christian living. Daniel Day fights back against the sins of excess, comfort, and apathy that so often permeate the American Christian worldview. His bold ten-day experiments shed light on the simple things we take for granted, and his experiences from around the world will inspire you to live your life differently."

— JUSTIN ZORADI, founder and CEO of These
    Numbers Have Faces and author of *Doing Work
    That Matters: A Small Guide to Making Big Change
    in the World*

"We at International Justice Mission are so grateful for friends around the world like Daniel Day—friends who live out what they believe. The world changes because of them. I hope you'll be inspired by Daniel's passion in these pages and follow him into taking action that makes a difference."

— GARY HAUGEN, president and CEO, International
    Justice Mission

10 DAYS
WITHOUT

FOREWORD BY **JONI EARECKSON TADA**

10 DAYS
WITHOUT

DARING ADVENTURES IN DISCOMFORT THAT WILL CHANGE YOUR WORLD AND YOU

DANIEL RYAN DAY

MULTNOMAH
BOOKS

TEN DAYS WITHOUT
PUBLISHED BY MULTNOMAH BOOKS
12265 Oracle Boulevard, Suite 200
Colorado Springs, Colorado 80921

All Scripture quotations, unless otherwise indicated, are taken from the Holy Bible, New International Version®, NIV®. Copyright © 1973, 1978, 1984 by Biblica Inc.™ Used by permission of Zondervan. All rights reserved worldwide. www.zondervan.com. Scripture quotations marked (NLT) are taken from the Holy Bible, New Living Translation, copyright © 1996, 2004, 2007. Used by permission of Tyndale House Publishers Inc., Carol Stream, Illinois 60188. All rights reserved.

Details in some anecdotes and stories have been changed to protect the identities of the persons involved.

The mention of organizations and/or websites in this book does not imply endorsement by WaterBrook Multnomah, Random House, or Ten Days Without.

Trade Paperback ISBN 978-1-60142-467-9
eBook ISBN 978-1-60142-468-6

Cover design by Kristopher K. Orr

Published in the United States by WaterBrook Multnomah, an imprint of the Crown Publishing Group, a division of Random House LLC, New York, a Penguin Random House Company.

MULTNOMAH and its mountain colophon are registered trademarks of Random House LLC.

Library of Congress Cataloging-in-Publication Data is on file with the Library of Congress.

Printed in the United States of America
2013—First Edition

10 9 8 7 6 5 4 3 2 1

SPECIAL SALES
Most WaterBrook Multnomah books are available at special quantity discounts when purchased in bulk by corporations, organizations, and special-interest groups. Custom imprinting or excerpting can also be done to fit special needs. For information, please e-mail SpecialMarkets@WaterBrookMultnomah.com or call 1-800-603-7051.

*My one- and three-year-old boys have prayed for
this book every day. Every night before bed
they asked God, "Help Daddy write his book.
Give him strength. Give him wisdom."*

*To thank my boys, I asked them to
write the dedication for this book:
"Noah and Finley, what should Daddy
write as the dedication for the book?"*

"What's a dedication?" Noah asked.

*"A dedication is where I mention a few
special people in the front of the book."*

*Noah pondered this for a moment and then responded:
"Say: 'To Noah. Happy birthday.
I love carrots, and I love racing.'"*

"Okay. Finley, what do you want me to write?"

"Raisins. Strawberries."

⇥ ⇥ ⇥

Then the King will say to those on his
right, "Come, you who are blessed by my
Father; take your inheritance, the kingdom prepared for you since the creation of
the world. For I was hungry and you gave
me something to eat, I was thirsty and
you gave me something to drink, I was a
stranger and you invited me in, I needed
clothes and you clothed me, I was sick
and you looked after me, I was in prison
and you came to visit me."

MATTHEW 25:34–36

Contents

Foreword

Let's get back to the basics.

At one time or another, every Christian has longed to carve away the calluses and clutter of life, but really...do we have a clue what that means? For some, it's opting for a less expensive vacation, not dining out as often, limiting the number of hours spent at a computer, or cutting back on all those church committees we serve on. But honestly, are these the basics Jesus would have us focus on?

It's easy to imagine that we live the Christian life, but when's the last time you, like Jesus, actually had no place to lay your head? Or consider his directives in Matthew 5:39–42: "But I tell you, Do not resist an evil person. If someone strikes you on the right cheek, turn to him the other also. And if someone wants to sue you and take your tunic, let him have your cloak as well. If someone forces you to go one mile, go with him two miles. Give to the one who asks you, and do not turn away from the one who wants to borrow from you."

Come on, who really lives like this? Such a lifestyle seems implausible, and so we interpret his words in our own way, suggesting that Jesus was only speaking metaphorically. Well, even if he was, most of us live nowhere near that plumb line. Admit it. Few of us give others the shirts off our backs. And if handed a financial windfall? We probably would not donate most of it to Kingdom causes; instead, it would get quietly folded into the family budget in order to widen our margins of comfortable living. Sorry, but that's the way we're wired.

Yet please don't think this book *Ten Days Without* is about to scold you for not living like a Spartan. No one is going to wag a finger at you for not giving more or living on less. Rather, my friend Daniel Day leads us on a fascinating experiment of what it might actually look like to get back to the basics—and what he discovers is absolutely captivating, as well as intriguing!

The chapter that touched me the most? It's Daniel's account of going ten days without use of his legs. I've been a quadriplegic for over forty-five years, and I would be the last one to wish paralysis on another, but I totally resonate with the insights Daniel gleaned. "Going without," whether for days or decades, actually does move one from a self-centered faith to an others-centered faith, not to mention a deeper experience of needing God desperately.

It requires great spiritual discipline, as well as a consuming adoration for the Savior, to not become seduced by the wiles and ways of our culture. And the excellent book you hold in your hands can help you get attuned to those siren calls that so often drown out the Spirit's guiding whispers: *"This is what Jesus meant; this is the better way; this is how you are to live; just walk in it."*

So get ready to begin the journey of your life. Once you start reading *Ten Days Without,* you won't be able to put it down…or put up with anything less than the normal—or I should say the basic—Christian life.

Joni Eareckson Tada

Joni and Friends International Disability Center

Fall 2013

Introduction

Those of us who live in the Western world live in a culture of excess.

Turn on the TV, and you see it. Pick up a popular magazine, and you see it. Eavesdrop on conversations at a coffee shop, watch people at the local mall, examine social media posts from your favorite celebrity—the examples go on and on.

Most of us have never experienced true need, genuine poverty, or authentically painful hunger. Our needs are met. Many of our wants are satisfied too.

And as a follower of Christ, I am bothered by this more and more as I've gotten older. Do society's priorities match what Jesus wants us to desire and obtain? Would Jesus be pleased with our culture of excess? With all our wealth and stuff, can't we do more to help people less fortunate in this country and in developing nations around the world?

As Christians, it seems like we're called to live differently; but how can we amid all the excess of our culture?

These kinds of questions haven't always concerned me. I wasn't the kid who gave away all his toys to needy families or the high school guy who ate only stale bread to draw attention to global issues. I grew up in a Christian home, attended a Christian school, and was involved in church, but I always felt as if my life was meant for something more. I wanted to honor God by loving him and loving others, but I didn't know how to make a difference.

Then I came up with the idea of Ten Days Without. This is the story of how I abandoned certain "necessities" as a way to increase awareness and raise money for amazing organizations that were doing good things to help others. It was my way of saying enough is enough—it's time to stop talking and time to start doing.

But it's more than just my journey; it can be yours too. I'm no expert in solving world problems. I'm still trying to figure things out. I've simply tried something that has worked for me and for many other people (you'll read some of their stories along the way). I started a blog, did some crazy experiments, opened up my life and experiences to the world, and shared honestly about my struggle to make an impact for God.

Maybe you're dissatisfied too. Maybe you know that you're destined to be more than just another shopper at the mall and another consumer of all the latest gadgets. Maybe in the midst of excess, you can chart a different path that makes God smile and has a lasting impact on people's lives.

If you're ready for an adventure that will challenge you, stretch you, and surprise you, then keep reading. The stories you'll encounter are real. More importantly, so is the change I— and many other people—have experienced by simply going Ten Days Without.

What Is Ten Days Without?

> ➤ ➤ ➤ So you see, faith by itself isn't enough. Unless it
> produces good deeds, it is dead and useless.
>
> JAMES 2:17, NLT

Sometimes asking one little question can turn your world up-
side down.

"What if making a difference in the world is as easy as walking into a business meeting without shoes?" I asked my wife on a
warm fall day three years ago.

She and I had been sitting on our living room floor laughing
about a goofy image: a guy walking into a high-powered meeting
in New York City, wearing an expensive suit but no shoes. Blame
the caffeine rush. Or a series of sleep-deprived nights.

She asked me to explain what I meant.

"I feel like my life is all about me and not about God," I said.
"Yeah, I work for a ministry, but I feel like all I'm doing is marketing. I'm writing e-mails. Updating websites. Designing brochures.
But I don't feel close to God. I don't feel like my life is making a
difference. It's like I'm caught in some sort of vicious cycle that
keeps me from growing closer to God or making an impact in
issues that matter. How does my little marketing job make a

difference in the big issues like poverty or human trafficking? How does my life help people see God?"

"Okay, but how would walking into a business meeting barefoot solve those kinds of issues?"

Good question. I paused to consider how it *would* make a difference.

"Well, if I walked around barefoot in places where people normally wear shoes, don't you think they would notice and want to know what I was doing? It would spark some amazing conversations! I could give up wearing shoes for a set period of time. Every day I'd write about the experience on a blog and connect it with a real-world issue and an organization that fights that problem. And then I could challenge people to get involved with that organization."

"Do you think that would make a huge difference?"

"Well, I'd be raising money and awareness for an organization that provides shoes for kids who don't have any, so children around the world would get a pair of shoes. Yeah, I think it would make a difference!" I started to get excited about this seemingly ridiculous idea.

"Okay, but for how long would you give up shoes?" she asked.

"I don't know. Forty days is all over the place in the Bible. That seems like a spiritual number."

"You want to give up wearing shoes for *forty* days? How about you do it for a week?"

"But that seems too short," I said.

"What about ten days?"

"Perfect!"

And that's how Ten Days Without was born.

The next day, before anyone could douse the flames of this crazy idea with a cold bucket of reality, I created a blog, and within a week I had started the Ten Days Without Shoes experiment. When I call it an experiment, I'm not exaggerating. I didn't have time to think about whether it was a good idea or not. It was just an idea, and with the support of the ministry I work for, I went for it.

And the response amazed me. My newly launched blog (10dayswithout.com) received over two thousand views in the first month, so I kept going. What else could I go without? Soon I went ten days without furniture, legs, media, a coat, waste, speech, human touch—each experiment a response to a need that I cared about.

But this is where things get really exciting: along the way, I realized that other people could join the cause. I didn't have to be the only one going ten days without   teenagers and young adults and parents and pastors and all kinds of other people could do similar experiments to inform and engage the people in *their* world.

And when I say *they,* I really mean *you*! This whole adventure is all about you: how your life can be absurdly altered for God, how your ten day sacrifice can help people see God, how this challenge can help you grow closer to God as you experience for a few days what some people in this world experience every day.

If you say yes to Ten Days Without, you're saying yes to going ten days without something—maybe something I went ten days without or maybe something particular to your life, your community, your passion. If you're a youth worker or leader, it means engaging a group of teenagers or young adults in this adventure and encouraging them to take ownership of this exciting opportunity.

We'll dive into the details a little bit later, and you can learn more on the special website we've created for this book, 10dayswithout.com. But it's my hope and prayer that as you continue to read about my experiments, you will be challenged to join the journey. If you do, your life will never be the same.

THE POWER OF GOING WITHOUT

A youth group in Iowa decided to do several challenges with me. One student, an amazing guy named Justin, went all out. He did the experiments, blogged about them, and posted his blogs on Facebook to challenge other people.

One of the challenges Justin completed was Ten Days Without Speech—he didn't use his voice for ten days. Many people would struggle to go ten minutes without speaking! When he began his journey, he got a little bit of resistance from a Facebook friend who challenged Justin by asking, "Not using your voice is great, but wouldn't it be better to use your voice and tell people what you are doing?"

His friend had a point, but in this case I think the best answer is no. We live in a noisy world, where people constantly bombard us with words and messages. They want us to support a candidate or buy a product or boycott a store or read their deepest, darkest secrets through their favorite social media platform. Those moments happen so often that we can become adept at turning them down. We "listen" without "listening." (Sounds like what our parents said we did in elementary school, right?)

So how can we raise awareness for an important cause within such a loud environment? Clearly we need a *countercultural way* of grabbing people's attention. And what could be more countercultural than going without? I've identified three specific, powerful results from going without: you put your beliefs and faith into action, you move beyond "slacktivism," and you dispel the culture's myths.

Let's explore each of these.

You Put Your Beliefs and Faith into Action

Once upon a time, I was addicted to good intentions. It may not sound like a risky addiction, but it has some nasty side effects. Apathy. Procrastination. Cynicism.

My life was full of good intentions—those things we write down in journals and share with friends or family, the important ideas that make us feel good about ourselves, the things we know we're "supposed" to do as followers of Christ. But for too many of us, our good intentions never become good actions. Without action, good intentions don't move us forward, draw us closer to God, or make a difference in the world. Good intentions are cans of paint that could have become amazing works of art—but never did. (If you want to see a video about good intentions, visit 10dayswithout.com and click on "Videos.")

I enjoyed sitting with friends and talking about problems that we saw in the church or the world. But for some reason, I was a lot better at *talking* about problems than *doing* anything about them.

I would end up getting too busy or too distracted, or I just wouldn't care enough.

And I had a feeling that I was not alone. Maybe this perfectly describes your life too.

I wanted to turn my "ideas that could have meant something" into "actions that mean something." I was tired of just saying that I follow Jesus. I wanted to actually live it—to serve God with my life.

Of course, the thought of serving God can be scary. I mean, what if God calls you to a life of serving society's outcasts? What if God asks you to sell all of your possessions and give them to the poor? What if God sends you to a foreign, distant land—like Texas? (Just kidding, my Texan friends.) I think that's why I had avoided asking God where he wanted me to serve: I was scared of what he would say.

Because I had gotten stuck in fear before and stayed stuck for a long time, I wanted this time to be different. So for the first time in my life, I put away my need to figure everything out and decided to just try something—to experience something by living it. Risky move, right?

We often need to *feel* something to *believe* it. It's one thing to watch a video about a horrible problem in the world, such as poverty. It's another thing to not use your furniture for ten days so that you can experience what it's like to sleep on a hard floor without a mattress. It's one thing to sit around a coffee shop with friends and talk about the problem of homelessness. It's an entirely different thing to take a homeless guy out to eat—so that's exactly what I did (but that story comes in the Ten Days Without a Coat chapter).

The experiences of Ten Days Without caused me to become more aware and more motivated, and I believe the same thing will happen in your life.

You Move Beyond Slacktivism

I also wanted to make sure that I was not falling into the trap of slacktivism.

Ever heard of "slacktivism"? The term is a mix of *slacker* and *activism*. It's when you text ten bucks to the Red Cross for people affected by a deadly hurricane—while you're watching your favorite reality show from the comfort of your home. It's when you see a compelling viral video and then e-mail it to your friends or share it on social media—and feel better because you have "done something." It's when you connect with a really good cause by "liking" a fan page. It's the idea that you have somehow contributed to the greater good without actually doing anything.

In a way, slacktivism is better than doing nothing at all. But the subtle danger of slacktivism is that we can check "doing good" off our spiritual or global-citizen checklists—or feel like we are involved with a serious problem in the world—without any life change or real commitment or genuine sacrifice.

I realize some people could argue that Ten Days Without is a new form of slacktivism. After "ten days of suffering without shoes on our carpeted floors," we somehow feel like we are done. We've put in our time to making the world a better place. We've fought poverty head-on, and we can go back to our normal lives again. But after doing so many different Ten Days Without experiments, I don't think that's possible.

When your heart, mind, soul, and strength work together for a cause, your life will change. Ten Days Without is built on the premise that it's better to get out of the coffee shop and do something, even if we don't have it all figured out. It's where our good intentions end and making a difference begins.

You Dispel the Culture's Myths

Our consumer culture is built on two basic myths: newer and bigger are always better, and wealth equals happiness. The best way to respond to these myths is to rebel. Yep, you read those words correctly. It's time for a little God-honoring rebellion.

Think of it as a personal insurrection of sorts, a rebellion against a culture that is always preaching "more" and "with." Going without is a way to experience change in our lives. And it's a way of learning humility.

During my time without shoes, one night my wife and I went out to eat before catching a movie. As we walked up to the restaurant, I noticed that my wife, who was also without shoes, was hesitant about going inside.

"What's up, babe?" I asked.

She looked at me with a nervous smile and whispered, "I feel like I am wearing my feet on my head!"

It's awkward to break social norms and go against everything that we are taught in our Western culture. But as we sacrifice these small, silly things, we are open to change in ways that we would never have been otherwise.

Here's how I look at it: this is similar to the spiritual discipline of fasting from food. (Yeah, I'm not always a big fan of that word *discipline* either—or of missing meals!) Fasting says, "Feel the pain of hunger, and it will remind you to pray or meditate on Scripture more." Ten Days Without says, "Feel the discomfort so that you can care and give more." Sometimes the pain is physical (hot asphalt on bare feet) and sometimes it's emotional (getting stared at or laughed at); but either way, it helps you think about these causes in a new light.

IT DOES MAKE A DIFFERENCE

Does sacrificing a "necessity" really make a difference? You bet it does—even if it doesn't always *feel* like it. Poverty, environmentalism, hunger, disabilities, spiritual compromise, homelessness, and modern-day slavery are all complex issues that affect millions of people in this world. You won't find an easy fix (tough for us to acknowledge because of our microwave mentality and fast-food fanaticism), and each issue can feel overwhelming. But taking a step and doing something makes a difference—in *you* and in *other people* who now have coats or shoes or other necessities they didn't have otherwise.

Here are three specific ways you make a difference when you go Ten Days Without.

You Influence the People Around You

Whether you realize it or not, you have a personal platform. That is, every day you influence a lot of people: friends, family members, classmates, coworkers, teachers, bosses, social media contacts— the list goes on. (Don't worry—I'm not saying you should feel paranoid; just be aware!) Your influence, either for good or for bad, has the greatest impact on those closest to you. Many of them genuinely care about your thoughts or opinions on certain issues or topics, so seize the opportunity. Ten Days Without is all about inspiring others to pursue and support the things God cares about and to oppose and resist the things God hates. (And sometimes an experiment like this will move past your personal platform and end up on the news. That happened to me twice. But I will talk about that more in the Ten Days Without a Coat chapter.)

God cares about the different causes you'll read about in this book. In the gospel of Matthew, Jesus talked about feeding the hungry, giving drinks to the thirsty, welcoming in the stranger, clothing the naked, taking care of the sick, and visiting the prisoner. In James, we read about the value of caring for the orphan and the widow. These are exactly the people you can assist in your own Ten Days Without challenges.

You Can Raise Money for Worthwhile Organizations

Doing these challenges also makes a difference because you can raise money or resources for ministries, organizations, and people serving on the front lines of these issues. Doing Ten Days Without Speech allowed me to raise funds for International Justice Mission to aid in their efforts to rescue girls from the commercial sex trade. My Ten Days Without a Coat experiment led to dozens of local homeless people receiving coats for the winter.

For each experiment, I partnered with a strategic organization responding to a specific problem. The way I raised funds for these organizations varied, but I'll go into more detail in each chapter.

I have put on my website a list of amazing organizations that fight poverty, homelessness, slavery, disease, and many more issues.[1] You'll also learn a lot more about these organizations as you read through this book. Obviously, you are welcome to support the same organizations I used, but I also encourage you to partner with your own church or other organizations that you know are trustworthy and making a difference.

You Create Lifelong Awareness and Action

If you walk around without shoes, show up at school or work in a wheelchair, stop talking, or ask others not to touch you, people will notice. They will want to know what's going on and why you're doing what you're doing. Even if their only response is looking at you weirdly, you still will have given them food for thought.

When I stopped speaking for ten days, I carried a whiteboard around with me as a way to communicate with people. At the top of the board I wrote, "I'm not using my voice to be a voice for…" followed by a statistic about people enslaved around the world. On the day I wrote, "Two million children stuck in the commercial slave trade,"[2] I encountered a barista at a coffee shop who thought the experiment was interesting but clearly didn't know how to respond. (Can you blame her?) After I got my coffee and sat down at a table, I thought about what would happen next.

Most likely she turned to a coworker and discussed how weird I was. But perhaps the conversation kept going, and they talked about the message on the board: that there are two million children around the world stuck in the commercial sex trade. And maybe one or both of them looked on the Internet later to see if my facts were true—and how they could get involved in combating the problem.

(Along these lines, I encourage you to carry around some small cards to hand out that explain the cause and what you hope to accomplish. There is more on this in chapters 2 and 5.)

When you do something different, people notice. Each of the Ten Days Without challenges creates an opportunity to make other people think about and remember the cause for a long time—and, we hope, take action and make a difference.

But just as importantly, this adventure can create lifelong awareness in *you*! I don't respond the same way when I see someone asking for change on the side of the road—I feel a sense of compassion that wasn't there before. My heart is genuinely stirred when I see those TV commercials about starving children in third-world nations because I realize the money I frivolously spend on lattes each week could help one of those kids eat better, live better, and survive. I sometimes intentionally go silent for an hour or two, just to remind myself of those children stuck in the commercial slave trade.

This is my genuine prayer for you: I want you to see the world differently after you do one or two or a dozen challenges. But don't just be aware—act! I'm reminded of something I've heard from many pastors who've taken teams of teenagers or young adults on mission trips. Sure, they accomplished something meaningful in the country they visited, but the biggest change happened in the lives of the people who went. But if all they did was just become aware and not commit to a lifetime of sharing the good news of Jesus, serving the needy, and ministering to people in their world, then the story isn't complete. Action must follow awareness.

How You Can Do This

Right now you might be ready to do this—to plunge into this exciting new adventure. You also might feel overwhelmed and intimidated—this will require some courage and boldness. I'll go into more detail near the end of the book, but here are four important steps as you move forward.

Pray

Pray for God's clarity and focus as you read this book, discuss it with friends, and then go without. Pray that God would open your eyes to the needs of the world, including needs I don't directly discuss in these pages. Pray that God would fill you with an amazing measure of compassion and love for people in need. Pray that God would give you powerfully creative ideas on how your excess could benefit people who lack. Pray that your life would never be the same after you take on some of these challenges.

Read

I don't want this to be the kind of book where you read about my experiences, get some feel-good emotions about helping people in the world, and then move on with your life. As you read these chapters, imagine yourself in my shoes. (Except when I talk about going without shoes—then imagine what it feels like to go without!) See if you're captivated by one of the challenges I discuss. Read with a prayerful attitude, asking God to reveal ways you can put these ideas into practice in your own life, your own sphere of influence.

Discuss

Don't do this as a solo adventure. Gather with a group of friends or your Sunday school class or your small group or your family or your entire youth group. Discuss the ideas in this book. Talk about what I did and what you'd do similarly—or differently! I think you'll find it easier to make it through the experiments if you have others around you who are also participating in them at the same time.

Go Without

Once you've prayed, read, and discussed, keep the adventure moving. It's time to go without something. Choose an issue, do some research, decide what you'll go ten days without, look for ways to partner with a ministry or organization, tell others what you're going to do, and then do it!

Ten Days Without is a chance to move beyond dialogue and good intentions, a way to make a difference in your community, your nation, and your world. Your life will change as you experience and understand these issues better and as you rebel against the social norm of consumerism through the ancient art of fasting—going without.

You have a powerful, God-given opportunity to make a difference by influencing the people around you. As you embark on this journey, not only will you open up yourself to new adventures and understanding, but you will also make a meaningful difference in people's lives.

Are you ready? Let's begin!

2

Your Soles Reflect Your Heart

Ten Days Without Shoes
to Address Disease

➤ ➤ ➤ Praise the LORD, O my soul, and forget not all his
benefits—who forgives all your sins and heals all
your diseases, who redeems your life from the pit
and crowns you with love and compassion.

PSALM 103:2–4

My name is Daniel Day, and I'm going ten days without shoes to provide shoes for children around the world who don't have any. For the next ten days I will be barefoot, period. If a store or restaurant doesn't allow people without shoes into its establishment, I will respect its policies and go elsewhere. Ten days. No shoes. Starts now.

Day 1…I had never realized how dirty gas stations were until I pulled up to one this morning. It's a beautiful day—yet the residue of gas lingers on the concrete and now on my feet. *My feet smell like gas!*

I didn't notice the smell right away. It took driving for

about a mile or two for the stench to waft up from the floorboards. As I continue driving toward work, I roll down my window to let in some fresh air.

As I slow down and pull up to my office building, the fresh air that was blowing through the window fades, and I can once again smell the petroleum clinging to my feet. Quickly, I get out of my car and pull my backpack out of the backseat. The asphalt is both hot and sharp, but being my first day without shoes I ignore the discomfort and head inside for another day in the office.

You would think that standing barefoot at a gas station would be about the worst it would get, but smelly feet is only the beginning of my adventures today. After a couple of hours at my desk, it's time to use the men's room. I get up from my nice comfy office chair and walk toward the public restroom in the middle of the building. For the first time since taking this job, I notice the soft, lumpy carpet beneath my toes. I swing open the restroom door, but my feet don't move. Slowly the door passes in front of my eyes and closes back in front of me. I swing it open again, and plant one of my bare feet on the ice-cold tile floor. But cold tile was the least of my problems! *Why am I doing this again?*

That was the day I truly valued shoes for the first time in my life—not as a status symbol or as a fashion statement or as an essential piece of athletic gear, but as a critical piece of clothing that protected me and kept me clean.

WE ARE DROWNING IN SHOES

How many pairs of shoes do you own? Not sure? Stop reading, set this book aside, and go to your closet. Count how many you own, and grab a pair. (Don't worry if it takes you a while; I'm not going anywhere!)

Okay, welcome back. (Seriously, you *did* go count your shoes and bring back a pair, right? Good!) So, how many do you own? It's probably more than you actually need—for some of us, the number is *way* more than we need! I love the video created by the shoe charity Soles4Souls about the shoe "problem" that we face every day.[3] Many of us resemble the shoe addict who jokes about needing to stop herself from buying so much footwear. Or the girl who exclaims, "I love shoes!" as clip after clip shows closets full of shoe collections.

Let's be honest: our shoe "problem" is ridiculously absurd. While getting dressed for a special occasion, have you ever asked yourself, "Which *pair* of black shoes do I want to wear?" Have you ever walked into a sporting goods store because you wanted to "get into hiking again" but didn't have a good pair of hiking boots because it's been months or years since you last trekked into the mountains?

Have you ever told your mom that you "needed" that over-priced pair of sneakers before the first day of school? Have you ever justified spending a lot of money on athletic shoes because they are better for your ankles, feet, or ball control? These are the shoe "problems" most of us face in our society of excess.

For us, shoes are fashion statements, athletic companions,

and creature comforts. They're reminders of how we live in a culture of countless choices. (Ever seen how many kinds of peanut butter the typical grocery store sells? Seriously—peanut butter!)

But in developing nations, kids need shoes because they don't have any, and they need shoes so that they don't get sick or so they can attend school. While we are looking for the right pair of shoes and complain because our brand-new shoes got dirty, they just want *a* pair of shoes. While we throw away seven hundred thousand tons of footwear and apparel every year,[4] children in other countries who are lucky enough to have a single pair of shoes are wearing literal holes in their soles.

And it's not just developing countries that have a need. There are many people in the United States who also need shoes because they don't have any. They are facing a *real* shoe problem.

If you join me for the Ten Days Without Shoes challenge, be prepared: you won't look at your life the same way when you're done. You won't be okay with owning twenty pairs of shoes. It won't be because of guilt—Ten Days Without is not about guilt—but because you will care about bigger, more important things than whether or not these loafers go with those trousers.

MY TEN DAYS WITHOUT SHOES

Confession time: going ten days without shoes was *disgusting.* Gas stations, public restrooms, parking lots, playgrounds, restaurants, and sticky movie theaters presented obvious hygiene issues. Not only was the experience disgusting, but it was also painful—like the day I went golfing barefoot. The nice soft grass would have been quite delightful if my golf skills allowed me to travel in the fairway. But no, that's not how I golf. Eighteen holes on the course means a minimum of eighteen trips into the rough—and a scorecard that looks like I played an NBA game, not a round of golf.

The next day, my feet looked like they'd survived a journey across a harsh desert or an intense rock climb. This is how I described it on my blog:

> My feet are still sore from yesterday. I can feel bruises in both the heel and the ball of my right foot. My left foot isn't bruised, but the skin is cracked where my big toe meets the rest of my foot. Every time I get up on my tippy-toes to reach something, I can feel the skin stretch and break a little more.[5]

Looking back, walking on the rough of a golf course gave me a taste of what it's like to be barefoot in a country where walking is a way of life. Most people in the developing world don't walk out of a carpeted home, get into a carpeted and climate-controlled car, and drive to a carpeted office building. They walk barefoot—everywhere!

In our culture, of course, going barefoot is taboo. Sure, it's okay at home. Maybe in the park for a few minutes. The community pool before and after a swim—that's fine. But when was the last time you saw someone walking around a mall without shoes? What would you think if one of your coworkers or classmates showed up barefoot tomorrow? This challenge forced me into a culturally uncomfortable spot—and it'll do the same for you too.

Some restaurants, stores, and gas stations require that customers wear shoes for service—sometimes because of health or safety standards and sometimes just because it's store policy. I decided that it would be wrong to violate those policies just because I was supporting a good cause. Ten Days Without is about lovingly drawing people's attention to important causes, and having a manager yell at me, kick me out, or threaten to call the cops isn't the kind of attention I wanted.

Fortunately, a lot of people in my sphere of influence became aware of what I was doing and why I was doing it—the right kind of attention! I organized a shoe drive and raised $171 to buy more shoes for kids. And I was terribly convicted by the amount of excess in my life. I walked through each room of my house, pulling out every pair of shoes I could find, collecting them on the bedroom floor. The pile was ridiculous—a mound of shoes that I had never worn or had worn only once.

Excess—you'll become more and more aware of it when you go ten days without. And once you realize how many people in the world live with so much less, you'll become even more passionate about using your stuff, your resources, and your blessings to meet their needs.

ENCOUNTERING THE PROBLEM IN HONDURAS

Going without shoes helped me discover the connection between being shoeless and the issues of poverty and disease, but the issue hit me harder several months later when I traveled to Honduras with Compassion International. The discomfort and grossness of walking barefoot into a gas station bathroom was insignificant compared to the genuine crisis I encountered in this Central American nation of eight million people. I also realized that any contribution I made was well worth any sacrifice.

As we traveled to a village in the mountains of Honduras, the bus was loud, both inside and out, bouncing down the gravel road. Strangers a mere twenty-four hours earlier, everyone was talking to each other as if we'd been friends for a long time. Half-listening to what my seatmate was saying, I was distracted by the countryside passing by the window. One of the translators noticed my focus on the nasty brown river rushing in the valley. He leaned over and said, "All the kids swim in that river."

"Seriously?" I half asked, half stated.

"Yep."

"Wow, that's gross," I said, turning back to the window.

I love rushing water, especially in the mountains, and even more so if there is a rock or a rope swing to jump off into the icy water. But you couldn't have paid me to get into that river. It looked like a sewer, a river of roaring brownish muck.

As the bus bounced back and forth down the road, I noticed an old, rusted-out suspension bridge stretching across the valley. It was about forty feet above the rushing water. I couldn't believe that it could still be in use, yet people were walking across it.

The bus slowed down, and the leader of our trip announced that we would be getting out. *Surely we are not walking across that bridge!* I thought. *It looks like a stunt bridge from an Indiana Jones movie!*

The bus driver opened the door, and one by one we filed out.

As bad as the bridge looked through the bus window, it looked even worse up close. Five thick metal wires were linked together by rotting boards and chain-link fencing. The hundred-yard-long bridge was filled with broken and splintering boards with rusty nails.

We decided that it would be best to cross the bridge one person per ten feet or so. I wanted to get it over with and volunteered to be one of the first to start across. (That was either genius or insanity!) The bridge creaked and moaned. I picked every step carefully, testing each board before placing my faith in its ability to hold me. Each additional person stepping onto the bridge made it sway a little more. When I got to the halfway point and looked down through the massive holes at the rushing river below, the bridge was swaying like a boat on three-foot seas. I grabbed both handrails and started sliding my hands along to keep from falling. The palm of my right hand snagged on a piece of rusty metal. It wasn't a big cut, but I couldn't help but worry that I would get tetanus.

As I reached the end of the bridge, I heard a crowd of excited children. I looked up to see fifty or more smiling faces yelling, *"Bienvenidos! Buenos días!"* ("Welcome! Good morning!")

"Buenos días!" I answered, as the children gave me high-fives and nervous smiles. I attempted to speak to them in my broken Spanish; their reactions made it clear that I still needed to work on it.

That's when I noticed a couple of the kids and some of the adults with bare feet. Their toes were covered in grime, their toenails broken and dirty, and their feet wrinkled from being exposed to the elements. Not only do these people walk around the rocky hillside of Honduras barefoot, but they also walk across that bridge with nothing to protect their feet from the rusty nails and splintering boards. Suddenly, my small experiment of going ten days without shoes didn't seem that small. Who knows—one of the kids there that day might have received a pair of shoes from the shoe drive I did several months before!

WITHOUT SHOES, DISEASE EASILY SPREADS

About three hundred million children around the world don't own a pair of adequate shoes.[6] Every day, they walk over rough terrain—on rocks, thorns, or bridges like the one I had to cross in Honduras—without anything to protect their feet. Every scratch, cut, thorn, or cactus needle presents a serious risk of infection or a way for a nasty disease to enter their frail bodies. This is especially true in communities where indoor plumbing does not exist. (In other words, that's not just mud they're stepping in.)

When I was walking through that small village in Honduras, I was shocked by the lack of sanitation. Even with shoes on, I planned each step carefully, not wanting to step on trash, used diapers, or anything left behind by the numerous dogs sniffing around. But the children around us didn't pay any attention to where they stepped. The boy I was following up to the church kicked every piece of trash that he found along the way while also stepping in every puddle. He was doing what my two-year-old son does whenever we walk through our quiet subdivision back home—only this boy didn't have any shoes to protect his feet.

Earlier I asked you to grab a pair of shoes from your closet. Look at those shoes right now. What's their story? How long have you owned them? How much did they cost? Where have you worn them? Hold a shoe in your hand. It's one of many shoes that you own, yet to a child, teenager, or adult living in a developing nation, you're holding something valuable and life giving.

Most developing countries face the perilous combination of malnutrition, lack of sanitation, and limited expert medical assistance. While in Honduras, I met a boy with a nasty scar on his wrist and palm. A few months earlier he had tried to climb a gate into a church. He had just made it to the top of the gate when he slipped. For several minutes, he was hanging there from the gate, his hand impaled by an iron spike.

Someone passing by noticed the dangling child, pulled him off, and bandaged his arm. The hole in his hand, however, was gaping and needed emergency medical attention. The father didn't have money to send his son to the hospital, but he received care through a Compassion International–sponsored program. Without that care, he likely would have died because of the infection.

But even preventable diseases can become life threatening. Some of the leading causes of disease in the developing world are soil transmitted. Diseases such as tetanus, hookworms, and podoconiosis are almost entirely preventable by wearing shoes, yet many children in the developing world will become seriously ill this year because they came into contact with one of these diseases through bare and cracked feet.

A lack of shoes also can impact a child's ability to go to school. In many developing countries, shoes are a required part of a student's uniform. Without shoes, children can't go to school, and then they lose their ability to break the cycle of poverty in their family. Instead of getting an education, they do things the same old way that the generations before them have always done them, therefore continuing the pattern of poverty.

But it doesn't have to be that way, because you can do something about it. You can remove a barrier that keeps children from going to school, and you can prevent them from getting terrible diseases.

Did you ever think a pair of shoes could so radically change a life?

STORIES FROM OTHER ADVENTURERS

You've heard a lot about what I saw and felt and learned, but I'm not the only person who's gone ten days without shoes. Many other people have joined this adventure and have shared their stories on my blog. Maybe your experience will be similar to what Lisa, a Ten Days Without Shoes participant, wrote:

I am so looking forward to wearing more comfortable shoes for daily life, gym shoes for walking, and pretty shoes for work. [The Ten Days Without Shoes experiment] has made me more aware of the things I do have in life. It's easy sometimes to think I have nothing, but the real reality is I am so very blessed. I'm thankful for all the options I'm afforded each and every day, from when I get dressed in the morning to what I decide to eat for meals.

Here's what Tamara, a mom in Iowa, said about her experience:

> I'm still embarrassed by the amount we "need" [after giving away our excess]: hiking shoes, running shoes, working-in-the-yard shoes, black dress shoes, and sandals—and that's just the boys. They each have five pairs of shoes. Annie has eight pairs, including slippers, and I have fourteen remaining "must haves." Maybe after a few more days without I'll be able to share a few more.

She also offered a poetic approach to explain the discomfort she felt during the challenge:

> Skin on scorched asphalt
> burns while loading bags in trunk.
> Thank you, cool shadow.
> Blacktop burns,
> cement warms,
> pine needles needle,
> the garage needs sweeping.
> My feet now speak to me in tones both subdued
>   and wrapped with irritation.

She wasn't the only person who experienced pain or disgust during the experiment. Here is how Daniel, a guy from Oxford, England, described day three of his Ten Days Without Shoes experience:

Getting colder in the city, it is harder to go about without shoes. This morning, I walked to Christ Church like I do every morning. There are a couple of graveled stretches of the walk that last about a hundred yards each. When I arrived in town, I rounded a corner and my knee buckled against my will. My leg had reacted to stepping on a small shard of glass before my brain could register what had happened.

I limped over to one of the benches on the sidewalk and examined the ball of my toes to find blood flowing freely. It wasn't a large piece of glass so it wasn't detrimental to my foot. It didn't look too bad so I kept walking to my school, which [was] about a quarter of a mile away. However, I found that walking on an open wound doesn't do much to help that wound heal. It bled for a good while.

Later on, I walked home from a party at the local Anglican bishop's house. The walk is a little over a mile and it began to rain about halfway there. The worst places to walk were (ironically) under bridges or overpasses, which I have to cross no matter which way I take home. The water flooding the ground mixed with the sewage that gathers at the low spots of the underpasses were unavoidable. My foot began to sting because the grime had entered my cut from earlier that day. Who knew such a minor injury could be such a nuisance?

If you do this challenge, you also will experience pain and discomfort, but I suspect you'll still say that it was worth it—not just because you'll be reminded of how nice and convenient it is to have a pair of shoes, but also because you're doing it on behalf of little lives.

Surprisingly, the most excited person to attempt Ten Days Without Shoes was a pregnant mom, Vianca, from Nashville, Tennessee. The moment she stumbled upon the blog and found out that three hundred million children around the world didn't have a pair of adequate shoes, she was hooked. As the mother of four kids, she could imagine what those barefoot children in the developing world go through. Here is what she wrote on day one of her journey:

This afternoon I began my journey to move on behalf of little lives! I was excited and enthusiastic, and then I left the house. My three-year-old daughter quickly wanted to know why I had forgotten something we never leave the house without: my shoes! After explaining to her about Ten Days Without Shoes she said I could [give away] some of her shoes. "Those little ones need them!" she said.

Upon arriving at my destination I came to realize how preconditioned we are in America to respect people's decisions and not ask questions. So when I got funny looks, I began to share why I was barefoot. (I am also pregnant so I'm sure the possibility that my fat feet outgrew all my shoes crossed some people's minds.) Nonetheless, the concrete was rough but bearable, the carpet was dirty but tolerable, but the mulch at the playground was awful. It felt like little daggers in my feet.

I was only one hour into my journey and I was already
encountering pain. Then I saw my little one playing on the
playground with her shoes on and no worries. I was truly
humbled. I proceeded to the bathroom and was disgusted
at the experience; it filled my mind with thoughts of all
the filth that these little ones must step in with cracked
toes and broken skin.

When I talked to Vianca about this experience later, I asked
her, "Why did you get so excited about this? What was it that
made you want to go ten days without shoes?"

She said that when someone shares a need in the world with
her, she has to do something about it, even if it's small. At the end
of her experiment, she decided to donate the same amount of
money that she would normally spend on one pair of shoes. For
her that was forty dollars, which can provide between eight and
forty pairs of shoes for kids in the developing world.

TIME FOR ACTION

Your involvement literally can save a child's life in another country. Even if you don't have a large sphere of influence for raising
money, you can still make a big difference. The first time I did
Ten Days Without Shoes, I was able to raise $171 in online dona-
tions for the organization I was sponsoring. (For the record, I've
gone ten days without shoes twice and plan to make it an annual
event in my life.) At first, that didn't seem like much money, but
then I remembered that it takes just a few dollars to buy a pair of

shoes for a child. I was happy knowing that dozens of kids received shoes because of my crazy adventure.

Here are the key steps to follow:

Raise Funds or Collect Shoes?

Decide if you want to do a fund-raiser or a shoe drive. A fund-raiser would simply be using your personal platform (see chapter 1) to raise as much money as you can for those without shoes. A shoe drive means that you use your personal platform to collect as many gently used or new shoes as you can for those without shoes.

Choose Your Partner

Find an organization that you can sponsor and support wholeheartedly. Do a little research, and choose an organization that effectively provides shoes to people in need. (Visit 10dayswithout .com and click on "Partner Organizations" for some suggestions.) See if the organization accepts used shoes or just money. Some organizations buy new shoes for kids in need and seek only fundraisers, not shoe drives. And remember, if you are collecting actual shoes, you may have to pay to ship them to the organization's collection site if it is not local.

Get People Interested and Involved

Tell people what you are doing—and why you're doing it. Share it on all your social media pages, send out e-mails or letters, and explain how people can get involved in the cause. Print cards to hand out to curious observers who want to know more. (Visit 10days without.com for templates and click on "Promo Material.")

Tell Your Story

Create a blog and use it (or other social media) to talk about your adventures. Use the funny stories, painful experiences, and awkward run-ins to help your personal platform connect with the issue. Post your stories on your own blog or on 10dayswithout .com.[7] Use your experience to help others experience the problem and then do something about it. Be the intermediary between the organization and your friends and family. Collect the shoes or funds, and then send them to the organization.

Ten Days Without Shoes is not about jumping on a trend and thinking that we made a difference by experiencing what it's like to step on a thornbush. It's about fighting disease and providing shoes for people in need. It's about responding to Jesus's call to compassionately care for the most needy, the most vulnerable, the most at-risk in our world. When people have shoes, they're exposed to fewer diseases and they have a better chance of going to school and to work, producing a better quality of life.

You can make a difference in the world today. You don't have to be wealthy or old or have an advanced degree to fight disease. You just need a caring heart, a passion to use your influence for something bigger than yourself, and a willingness to try something different. Going ten days without shoes is a revolutionary way to put your faith into action.

3

Seeing Jesus on the Streets

Ten Days Without a Coat
to Address Homelessness

➤ ➤ ➤ Suppose a brother or sister is without clothes and
daily food. If one of you says to him, "Go, I wish
you well; keep warm and well fed," but does
nothing about his physical needs, what good is it?

JAMES 2:15–16

My name is Daniel Day, and I'm going ten days without a coat to provide coats for homeless people in my hometown. For the next ten days I will be coatless, no exceptions. Ten days. No coat. Starts now.

Day 8…Right now it's 4 degrees outside, with a wind-chill
temperature of -7 degrees. It's a great day to stare out the
window with a cup of something hot and delicious, but
not a great day to go outside without a jacket. Although
my mom would tell me not to leave the house without
covering my arms, I'm in the middle of Ten Days Without
a Coat and skipping work is not an option. I grab my

backpack, put on my snow boots (did I mention it's snowing as well?), and head out to the driveway to get into my car.

Goose bumps appear on my arms immediately, and neighbors look at me, concerned that I've lost my mind. I hit my door with a clenched fist because it is frozen shut, and I almost break my key as I try to unlock the door. I look like a smoker as every breath turns into a light gray cloud in front of my lips. I turn on the car, blast the heater, and step back out into the snow to scrape my windshield. When I get back into the car, the heat has still not kicked on, and I'm rubbing my arms as I shift into gear. After a long fifteen minutes, the air in the vents begins to turn warm, and by the time I get to the office I'm comfortable— just in time to get out of the car again!

Enduring Winter Without a Coat

Living in Colorado means enduring a few months of hard winter. But I really can't complain (even though I sometimes do). I have a warm house, a warm office, and a car that eventually gets warm if driven far enough. I have the money to eat in warm restaurants, and I buy lots of warm beverages to wrap my hands around. So why would I go without a coat for ten days in the middle of a Colorado winter?

I knew this was the right challenge when I heard that the local rescue mission needed five thousand coats, mostly for women and children. I know how cold it can get here in Colorado (if you live in Florida like most of my family does, just pretend you can relate), and the idea of people sleeping outside without a jacket sounded deadly—which it can be. So I decided to do a coat drive and see how many coats I could get donated by the end of ten days.

They say charity starts at home (though I'm not quite sure who "they" are), so I dug into my closet to hunt for any extra coats or jackets that I could donate. Not surprisingly, my hunt was successful. Here's what I wrote in my journal:

> I had a sneezing fit last night—all because of dust. I decided to pull out every coat that I own and count them, and evidently some of them have been in the back of my closet for a long time!
>
> I'm embarrassed to even admit this next part, but do you know how many coats I own? Eighteen! I pulled eighteen coats out of my closet. And then I decided to try them all on at the same time and videotape it.[8]

That evening, I decided that I didn't need eighteen coats; in fact, I decided to give away eleven of them because eleven people in my community needed coats more than I needed a closet full of them.

How many coats do *you* have? Take a few minutes right now to go around your home and round up all your jackets. If you're really adventurous, do what I did: place all your coats on the bed, and then try to put them all on at one time. Start with one, then add another on top of it, and another on top of that—and when you start to look ridiculous, stop and donate the rest!

Walking Outside in a Short-Sleeve Shirt

December brought its share of cold days and nights during this challenge; nighttime temperatures reached the single digits in Colorado Springs several times during my ten days without a coat. I discovered the misery of scraping snow off my car in a short-sleeve shirt. Several times I went out to play in the snow with my family—my bundled, jacketed, warm family!

No, I didn't spend a night sleeping under a bridge or staying in a shelter or experiencing some of the other daily realities for someone who's homeless. But my brief exposure to the problem made me appreciate something as simple as a coat in the middle of winter.

And I was pleased that a couple of days after I began my challenge, the local NBC and ABC news stations heard about the experiment and decided to cover the story, giving me the chance to talk about several of the challenges I'd done. And perhaps the most exciting moment of the challenge came when a woman I had never met stopped by the office and donated an entire bag of kids' coats. She was outside my personal sphere of influence but heard about the experiment on the news and wanted to help.

Ten Days Without a Coat is about the thousands of people who don't have places to live, who don't work in warm offices, who don't drive warm cars. They aren't meeting their friends at warm coffee shops or sitting in front of warm fireplaces with warm blankets and cups of hot chocolate. Instead, they are holding cardboard signs in snow-covered parking lots, sleeping under icy overpasses, or walking down windy streets—wishing they had another layer to add for warmth.

HOMELESSNESS IS A LOCAL PROBLEM
IN ALMOST EVERY LOCALE

You don't have to travel to another country to find people who are homeless—you may have to drive only a few minutes to enter their world. You may never witness the impact of helping orphans in a distant nation, but you can personally see the transformation when someone from your own community successfully transitions away from homelessness.

Larry Yonker, the chief development officer of Springs Rescue Mission told me, "The need for coats is higher than it has ever been here [in Colorado Springs] with the growing number of people out of work. Children's coats are the most critical because the kids grow out of them so fast… The fastest growing homeless population is women with children."

According to the National Alliance to End Homelessness, families with children make up 38 percent of the homeless population in the United States. In 2012, more than 630,000 people throughout the nation were homeless—nearly 100,000 of whom are considered chronically homeless (meaning they are homeless year in and year out).[9]

Without a home, people must find a substitute for shelter or face the elements. Cold nights pose perhaps the greatest risk, but rain and heat create their own share of problems. Plus, having a home can provide emotional stability and security. It's where you rest and unwind, where you entertain friends and celebrate family achievements. And think of your childhood memories of home: playing sports in the yard or baking cookies in the kitchen or snuggling with loved ones as you read books or watched favorite movies—even if you fumbled the football, burned the cookies, and watched the silliest movies!

Here's a big part of the problem: we don't know how to help the homeless. We care, we're compassionate, but giving spare change to a guy on a street corner doesn't feel like a real solution or answer. I've struggled with this. I remember being in a coffee shop with some friends and seeing a homeless guy sitting on the street outside. We spent the rest of our time talking about the need to help other people. Yet we left without reaching a conclusion or concocting a plan—and the homeless guy was still sitting there, lonely, neglected, and hungry.

We don't have to live this way! We don't have to live our lives avoiding the homeless because we don't know how to help them. With a little bit of knowledge and a willingness to try something new, you can help the homeless in your community.

Caring with Pure Motives

The best gift you can give a homeless person is time without a hidden agenda. In his book *Under the Overpass,* Mike Yankoski talked about the experiences he and a friend encountered as they spent several months homeless in different cities around the country. One of my favorite parts of the book centers on an evening when a young woman took them to dinner, and the best part of that night was the conversation they had. The meal was great, and they needed the food, but they truly appreciated the conversation and her willingness to sacrifice some time for them.

Going ten days without a coat was a great first step to fighting homelessness, but for me it still wasn't enough. I realized that I needed to deal with some prejudice and fear deep inside me. Jesus was known, in part, for hanging out with the "untouchables" of society—and in my life, that group included people who were homeless. For me to care about them as people, I needed to get past my fear.

And I knew I wasn't the only one uneasy about interacting with the homeless, because my friend Brian shared a part of his story with me. Brian is one of those guys whom I have always looked up to because he seems so in tune with God. One day, I found out that his house was full of homeless people whom he had found on the street and invited to live with him.

Wow! How many of us would be willing to do that?

But a few months later, I found out that Brian was scared the first time he invited a homeless guy to stay at his house. Here's what he told me:

> [I recall] the first night I invited a guy right in off the street to live with me. He was what most people would call your typical homeless guy. He was socially awkward and just wanted to watch *Full Metal Jacket* a lot! I remember making us some hot ramen noodles that cold Sunday night in February, and we just watched the TV, and he told me about his political point of view. Then we headed

off to bed, and I played like I was fine, but I was scared out of my mind—*terrified,* in fact. I even pushed the chest of drawers in front of the door to keep him from coming in while I was sleeping. People joke about sleeping with one eye open—well, that night I did. But you eventually grow to love instead of fear. Now over a year later, I have two men who were homeless sleeping in the same *room* with me! God is good, and he works in love.

I'm not saying that we should all go downtown and offer up our homes like Brian did. We need to be wise, and part of being wise means being careful. But at the same time, we need to remember that "perfect love drives out fear" (1 John 4:18). We can't use our apprehension as an excuse to avoid people God cares about and loves.

And that's why I took Calvin out to lunch.

DINING WITH STRANGERS

I was genuinely apprehensive about walking up to a random homeless guy and asking, "Do you want to go to lunch? My treat!" Would he accept? Would he yell at me? Would he say yes but insist on eating at the most expensive restaurant in town?

He accepted my offer. He didn't yell at me. And he was fine with an inexpensive meal.

The day I put away my fear and ate lunch with Calvin turned out to be one of the best experiences of my life. The encounter challenged me and stretched me. He cussed a lot and started smoking weed at the end of my time with him—but he was also an all-around nice guy who needed a friend. That meal helped me remember that each person who's homeless is a person loved by God, a person who desires and needs connection with other people.

And going to lunch with him gave me the courage and inspiration to go back to a grocery store on a cold winter evening and meet a guy named Abraham.

Battling My Conscience

It was freezing outside. The temperature was in the teens, and snow covered the ground. I had just left the store and was headed home. As I sat at the stoplight, I noticed a guy with a cardboard sign huddled down in the median. The hood of his jacket was pulled up over his head, and he looked miserable. I felt something inside me say, "Stop and help him out." But I didn't want to give him money that would be spent on beer or drugs, so I ignored my conscience.

But the picture of that man was branded into my mind. *How was he going to stay warm?* When I got home, I dropped off the groceries in the kitchen and then walked back to the front door. My wife asked me where I was going, but before I could answer, my son interrupted and said, "Daddy, can I go?"

I grabbed my son's tiny jacket and put it over his shoulders while explaining to my wife why I had to leave. "Honey, tonight is going to be different. I am not going to once again be a victim to my own laziness and pride. I've got to help this homeless man."

As I soon discovered, Abraham was the name of that guy sitting outside the grocery store on that cold winter night.

Unsure What to Say

After I put my son in the car, I jumped in the front seat and began driving back toward the shopping center. The entire way there I was praying that God would show me an opportunity to help.

I pulled into a gas station adjacent to the shopping center and waited for a moment. Abraham was still at the corner, but I had no idea what to say to him. I sat in the car for what seemed like forever—planning my next move and waiting for the right opportunity. Before I had the chance to get out of my car, I noticed someone hand Abraham a wad of cash. As soon as the light turned green and those cars cycled away, Abraham stood up, walked right past my car, and went into the gas station.

I waited outside and watched him for a moment. He walked into the store, and I could tell that he was delaying his purchase to absorb a little extra warmth. But a couple of minutes later, he walked out—after purchasing two giant cans of cheap beer. I couldn't believe it—the stereotypical homeless guy buying beer! But I wasn't going to let my prejudice get in the way of helping him out.

"Excuse me," I said, after rolling down my window.

"Yes?" he asked. "What do you want?"

"I noticed that you were sitting on the street, and I was wondering if you would like a nice warm dinner?"

"Okay," he replied, but clearly he was doubting my good intentions and waiting for the catch.

"Pick any restaurant within driving distance, and I will treat you to dinner," I told him.

"I like the Chinese place."

"Chinese it is. Would you like a ride?"

"Sure."

And with that, a random homeless guy opened up the passenger-side door of my car, sat down, and slid his beer under his feet. That short drive felt like it lasted forever, filled with awkward silence. The only question I could muster was to ask him his name.

"Nice to meet you, Abraham. I'm Daniel, and that's my son Noah in the backseat."

We all got out of the car, and the three of us went into the Chinese restaurant, unsure what was supposed to happen next. I told Abraham to get whatever he wanted so that he could have food for the next day if he needed it. He took me up on my offer and ordered the most expensive item on the menu. When we were seated, I finally attempted a conversation.

Skeptical About My Generosity

"So what's your story, Abraham?" I asked. "Where are you from? Do you have any family?"

"I'm from California," he responded, "and I have a sister there. My mom lives here in the Springs. Are you a Christian?"

"Uh, yes," I replied, caught off guard by his question.

"I figured you were a Christian. They are the only ones who ever give me food."

Part of me was proud of the church that had obviously reached out to Abraham before; but another part of me caught something else in his voice: skepticism, as if he had just figured out the catch to my generosity.

"Are you going to tell me about Jesus?" he asked.

"No," I responded. "I'm only taking you out to eat. Besides, it sounds like you've already heard about him."

"Yeah," he said, still staring at his food.

It became obvious that Abraham had been treated to dinner a lot, but that he felt like there was always a hidden agenda. Recognizing this, I stayed away from any kind of religious conversation.

He told me about his mom and her new boyfriend and the fact that he wasn't allowed to stay with them until they moved into a new house. It sounded like he would be homeless for the next few days, so I offered to find him a shelter. He told me not to bother, but because of how cold it was outside, I called around anyway.

Nowhere for Him to Stay

Amazingly, I couldn't find one shelter that would answer the phone. Here was a guy who needed help, yet none of the places that could assist him were answering their phones. I knew for sure that I couldn't take him back to our house because my family was there.

But what could I do? I couldn't leave him outside all night!

I told Abraham that I was going to drive him downtown to whatever shelters we could find and that we were going to find a place for him to stay—but he wasn't interested. He asked me to drive him to the bridge where he sleeps and assured me that he had blankets and a warm jacket hidden in the trees. I couldn't help someone who didn't want to be helped, so I dropped him off at the bridge.

Before he got out, I told him that I would meet him at a local coffee shop the next morning and treat him to a warm cup of coffee and breakfast. He said, "Okay," and then disappeared into the darkness of the bridge. I drove away helpless but confident that I had done everything I could to help him.

I haven't seen Abraham again, but I'm always keeping my eyes open, just in case.

HANDLING DISAPPOINTMENT AND REDEFINING SUCCESS

Have you ever heard the cheesy starfish story? (No, the starfish wasn't cheesy; just the story!) It's the modern parable about an old man walking along the beach who sees a little kid trying to throw an entire colony of starfish back into the water, one at a time. The old man tells the kid there's no way he can make a difference because he can't throw them all back. Wisely, the child picks one up and says, "It matters to this one."[10] Well, by the end of my coatless time, I felt like the old man.

You see, of all the ten-day challenges I've done, going without a coat remains the most discouraging experience. My goal was to drop off five thousand coats—and I fell short of the goal. *Way* short of the goal. I don't know what the final number of coats was, but it was less than one hundred.

Sure, I could have focused on the positives: The local news had covered the story. A Sunday school class in North Carolina had taken the challenge. And enough coats were donated that I had to make two trips to the rescue mission to drop them off. But the weight of the need—knowing that I was unable to help thousands of people who needed coats—came crashing down on my shoulders. I felt like I had failed.

For the first time in my Ten Days Without journey, the magnitude of the problem seemed to dwarf my noblest efforts. My seemingly small and insignificant coat drive made little impact on the monstrosity of the problem of homelessness.

All the problems I have sought to address through Ten Days Without—such as disease, poverty, and homelessness—are huge. And yet here I am, one individual human being trying to "change the world." But can I really make a difference? The world is a huge place with huge problems. I can't even solve the problem of five thousand coats in my own community.

But Your Efforts Still Matter

Okay, time to hit the pause button on my soliloquy of sadness. I don't want my experience to discourage you, because despite my initial feelings of failure, I *did* learn a vital lesson in all this: you and I can make a difference, as long as we properly define what we're trying to accomplish.

Maybe you *can* collect five thousand coats. Maybe you *can* gather enough donations to feed a holiday meal to one thousand people. Maybe you *can* connect with a dozen employers in your community who will give a shot to fifty people who are homeless—a shot at a career, an income, and a way to provide for their families.

But even if you don't reach your goals, you'll make a difference. You'll become aware, and you'll help other people become aware too. You'll likely meet people who used to be homeless or who are looking for a way out. You'll know how to pray and serve and act.

And here's an important declaration that flows from the essential lesson I learned: I think it's risky to believe that it's our responsibility as individuals to change the entire world—and I'm not sure it's healthy to try. If we go at it with that perspective, we are setting ourselves up for failure and disappointment and frustration because the truly global problems are immense. One person alone cannot bring peace to the Middle East or solve world hunger or end homelessness.

But God does call us to make a difference in the world of the individual. If you can provide fifty or a hundred coats, you are doing something worthwhile because that's fifty or a hundred people who will be a little warmer this winter—fifty or a hundred people who can better endure the cold and the rain.

So maybe instead of trying to change *the* world, we need to focus on changing *someone's* world. For example, what if I had put a tracking device in one of my coats and was able to find the man or woman who received it? (Okay, that sounds really creepy— maybe the staff at the homeless shelter could just introduce me to that person.) What if I was able to ask what having a coat meant to that person? Perhaps he or she would respond by saying, "It meant the world to me." That one coat didn't change the world, but it did change *that person's world*! It's time to have the attitude of the starfish-throwing child.

That's what making a difference in the world means to me

now, thanks to the "failure" with my coat drive. I can make a big impact on our world's biggest issues simply by finding a way to change one individual's world—a noble goal to pursue each day.

And you can too.

TIME FOR ACTION

So how can you make an impact on homelessness?

Understand the Need

Visit a local rescue mission, ministry, or organization that actively assists people who are homeless. The staff members can speak knowledgeably about the greatest needs in your community and the most effective ways you can help address those needs. Ask them how you can get involved and truly make a difference.

Decide What You'll Give Up

Going without a coat is a great way to draw attention to the need for coats among people who are homeless, but if you want to create awareness about a different need, you may want to give up something else.

And if you live somewhere sunny—Hawaii comes to mind—then you might not need to distribute coats, but you can still find ways to help the homeless. You could go ten days without a car, drawing attention to how tough it is to walk or ride a bike everywhere in the heat. You could buy or collect water bottles, fill a cooler with them and some ice, and hand out ice-cold water to homeless people as you walk around town. The key is to be aware of the needs in your community and then be creative as you strive to meet those needs.

Create Your Plan

During my experiment, I encouraged people to donate their coats directly to a local rescue mission, a food pantry, or the Salvation Army. (Who knows—maybe my Ten Days Without a Coat challenge inspired a lot of people to make donations, but they never let me know!) And if they couldn't find a place to drop off their donations, they could mail them to me. Use whatever strategy works best—just make sure to have a strategy!

Spread the Word

Tell people what you're doing—and why you're doing it. Talk about it on social media, send out e-mails or letters, and let your friends, family, coworkers, and acquaintances know how they can get involved in the cause.

Deliver the Donations

Follow through on your commitment to getting the goods to the organization you are sponsoring. Collecting coats is great. Other means of involvement are great. But if you've collected items that are meant to help people, make sure they get to the organization or ministry!

Ten Days Without a Coat will introduce you to people you might normally avoid. It challenged me to pay attention to people I subconsciously had placed on my "untouchables" list. I don't know what impact I had on Calvin, Abraham, or the few dozen people who received a warm coat for the winter, but I know that I did *something*—my small part in trying to change their world. Maybe that's what it really means to make a difference in the first place.

4

Disconnect and Discover

Ten Days Without Media
to Address Distractions

➤ ➤ ➤ Since, then, you have been raised with Christ, set
your hearts on things above, where Christ is seated
at the right hand of God. Set your minds on
things above, not on earthly things.

COLOSSIANS 3:1–2

*My name is Daniel Day, and I'm going ten days without media
because I need a break from distractions and overload and I need
to refocus on important things! For the next ten days I will not be
watching TV, listening to music, using the Internet, playing video
games, looking at advertisements, or using my smartphone for anything other than making phone calls. Ten days. No media. Starts
now.*

Day 1…I have an addiction. It's not obvious to everyone,
just to those who know me the best. Lucky for me, this
addiction is neither illegal nor discouraged. In fact, billions
of dollars every year are spent on helping people like me

stay hooked. The addiction has gotten so bad that it's hard for me to even imagine life without this substance. And picturing life without it is like picturing a world of darkness without any fun or happiness.

What has me so wickedly trapped? Media.

My personal weakness is a little rectangular touchscreen in my pocket. My cell phone gives me immediate access to the latest fantasy football updates, my e-mail, YouTube videos, games, and all my music. I can check social media, watch a movie, download a random dog whistle, and manage my bank account. With the touch of a finger, I spend hours flipping through different apps or surfing the web. My addiction can be so bad that when I visit relatives in other states whom I haven't seen in several months, I will still spend most of my time on my phone.

So Ten Days Without Media is a personal detox as I attempt to free myself from media's stranglehold on my life. It's a personal insurrection against the system that says, "The more technology we can fit into our pockets, the better." It's a way for me to cut out this part of my life and see if there is a better way to live that's simply waiting for me to sign out of my news feed.

CAN YOU REALLY GO TEN DAYS WITHOUT MEDIA?

Before we go any further in this chapter, let me say something important: going ten days without all media is virtually impossible.

I recently heard a line in a movie that stuck with me. Here's my paraphrase of what was said in *The Greatest Movie Ever Sold:* "The only place where we can get away from advertisements is to go to sleep." I found this to be true during my media fast.

One morning during my ten days without media, I found what looked like a newspaper on my driveway, but it was just a bunch of ads folded up in a little orange plastic bag. I hadn't even left my house yet, and already someone had pushed advertisements in front of my face.

On my way to work, I was met with dozens of other ads—and that doesn't include the signs of all the stores I passed. The advertisements included billboards and banners and real-estate signs and seasonal promotions. I stopped by the grocery store and heard music that was interrupted by announcements for a sale on avocados. And then I went to the office filled with coworkers listening to music.

I thought about buying those bright orange earplugs construction workers use—at least they would have blocked out the sounds and noise. I didn't know what to do about visual "noise," though. I could have driven to work blindfolded, but other drivers wouldn't have appreciated that very much.

Perhaps we can never completely get rid of media regardless of our efforts to keep the TV off, the laptop closed, and the radio silenced.

Isn't that amazing? Even if we don't want to find media, media still finds us.

But going without media is still a beneficial challenge that's worth the sacrifice.

Rescuing the Smartphone Widows (and Widowers)

My media fast produced the truth about one of the deepest, darkest secrets in my family: my wife felt like a smartphone widow. All the time I spent using my phone to read e-mails, update social media, and check sports scores made her feel unimportant and unloved. I didn't realize it, but that's how she felt—like an iPhone, Facebook, and ESPN widow.

And it's not just young people who have this problem. (I'm in my twenties, so I'm going to call myself "young" for as long as my wife lets me!) I recently sat next to two older women in a coffee shop, one of whom was talking about her husband. "My husband hates the smartphone because he says if I'm not playing games, I'm checking e-mails." I couldn't help but smirk to myself. This lady was easily pushing seventy, and she spent too much time playing games on her smartphone! That's hilarious—except that it's actually not funny. Excessive media consumption can divide families and distract people from spending time with the ones they love. My wife felt like a widow, and this woman's husband felt like a widower. Sad.

What form of media represents your greatest weakness? Are you like me, tethered and tied to your smartphone all day? Does your couch have a permanent sag because of all the hours you sit on it watching TV? Maybe your time is consumed by video games or social media or texting or music. Try this: Keep a media journal for the next week. Track which media you consume and how much time you spend with it. At the end of the week, go back and add up the totals. Then ask God for forgiveness for all the wasted time. Just kidding—or maybe not.

I also invite you to ask some of the significant people in your life to see what they've noticed. If they're like the significant people in *my* life, they'll gladly tell you what's robbing them of meaningful time with you!

I experienced some amazing benefits from my ten days without media. Instead of listening to music on my phone or computer or digital player, I created some by playing the guitar and piano. Instead of watching movies or television shows, I read the Bible for the first time in a long time. And my wife loved the fact that because I couldn't use my smartphone, we spent lots of quality time together.

That's really what this challenge is all about. Unlike most of the other experiences in this book, fasting from media isn't about supporting an organization to address a global epidemic. Instead, it's about each of us doing our part to address a different kind of problem: relationships. Your family and friends want and need to spend more time with you, even if they haven't said it directly—or posted "I miss you!" on social media because they know that's the only way you'll see it!

THE REWARDS OF A MEDIA FAST

We live in a media-saturated world. It wakes us up in the morning, accompanies us to school or work, helps us get our workloads done, offers breaks during the day, connects us to all our friends, accompanies us home from school or work, entertains us before bed, sings us to sleep, and sometimes wakes us up in the middle of the night. It's virtually impossible to escape and requires a lot of effort to ignore. Most of us have welcomed technology into our lives and homes without ever considering a very important question: Is it good for me?

According to the Kaiser Family Foundation, every day the average teenager consumes over ten hours of media, including seven-and-a-half hours of uninterrupted usage (meaning they're multitasking with multiple media forms for part of the day).[11] How do teenagers spend that time? The list includes things like TV, movies, music, print, Internet, and video games. Isn't that crazy? Over a third of the day devoted to media consumption— that's more than an entire school day!

Media is filled with ideas, and ideas have consequences. If we believe something is true, it can change our lives for the better or worse. Media's real power and brilliance come in the *way* it teaches ideas. Tell me a random fact about monkeys during a routine conversation, and I probably won't remember it the next day. Put a random fact about monkeys into the melody of a catchy song, and I will be singing it before the song ends. And if my young children hear the song, we'll all be singing it that night. And in the morning. And every time we're in the car. And every time we're playing in the yard. And—well, you get the idea.

We need to be aware of the messages we are consuming when we watch a television show, go to a movie, or listen to music. We need discerning hearts and minds when we open a magazine or read a book. As Paul put it, we either take thoughts captive or we are taken captive by them. (Check out 2 Corinthians 10:5 and Colossians 2:8.) And please understand that when I talk about the problem of media, I am not saying that all media is bad. I am saying that the unbridled consumption of media is bad.

My own experience turned me into a big fan of going ten days without media. It's a worthwhile and beneficial challenge that forces us into some unfamiliar but rewarding situations.

You Can Focus on Nobler Tasks

Most people want to make a difference in the big issues of our world, whether it's poverty, human trafficking, slavery, or homelessness. They strive to lead lives that count, and they want to change the world. But many of those same people also spend a lot of time watching their favorite TV shows or playing video games or following their sports team's every game or checking every bank transaction and every nugget of news. In many ways, media keeps people from living for something bigger than themselves. Media has become a diversion, an interruption, a disruption.

I already confessed to being a media addict, and going ten days without media helped me discover how much of my life is consumed by distractions. But it doesn't have to be this way. We can choose how we use our time. (Seriously, has anyone ever *forced* you to watch hours and hours of TV every night?) We can choose to spend our days pursuing significant goals and doing things that truly matter.

You Can Practice Creativity

It's no exaggeration to say that many of us have no idea what to do when our phones are out of range or the Wi-Fi stops working.

(Think about the last time it happened to you; didn't you panic just a little bit?) Our creativity has disappeared—at least, that's what Warner, a twelve-year-old boy from Iowa, admitted on day one of his experiment without media:

> If you had asked me before today if I used media a lot I probably would have said no. But after today, I have realized how much I actually use it. I don't think going without media would have been so hard today if the weather wasn't so soggy. I constantly caught myself looking at my phone or going to Facebook without even thinking about it. I spent a lot of the morning sitting in my room thinking about what I'm going to do for the next ten days. I can tell this is going to be a very testing challenge.

Media is a great way to avoid getting bored, but contrary to what many of us think, boredom isn't always a bad thing. In September 2012, CNN hosted an article on its website titled "Have Smartphones Killed Boredom (and Is That Good)?"[12] The article describes today's current media-centric culture and cited a study done by the Social Issues Research Centre in Oxford, England. The study's main point: smartphones have replaced the time that we would normally be bored—time we would spend on personal thought, reflection, or simply zoning out. These days, when a light turns red or we are waiting in a line for coffee, we are on our phones checking e-mail or scores, playing games, or texting. We have no more downtime. Just look around you next time you're at a stoplight or in the store to see how preoccupied we are. It's crazy.

The research center points out the key role downtime and boredom play in fueling creativity. We have all experienced this to one extent or another. You know how people seem to say that the best ideas come to them in the shower? Maybe that's because we leave our smartphones on the counter! (Well, most of us do.) The shower may be the only place most of us get away from media—unless, of course, you listen to music when you bathe.

God creatively created you to be a creative being! We all benefit from creativity. We need to be creative at our jobs and in our schoolwork. We seek to be funny and original and entertaining—traits that rely on creativity. Set the noise and distractions aside, and let your mind wander. Embrace boredom and silence, and let your brain do its thing.

You Can Rediscover Simpler Pleasures

Media also can slowly erode our ability to enjoy simple pleasures. It's a phenomenon called *anhedonia,* which means "the loss of pleasure," or joylessness and cheerlessness. This concept is talked about in detail in Dr. Archibald Hart's book *Thrilled to Death.* Hart, a psychologist, discussed the pleasure center of the brain and the effect of constant media exposure. He described the pleasure center of the brain as being like "a barrel without a bottom—it never gets full. The more you give it, the more it wants."[13]

According to a TED talk given by psychologist and professor emeritus at Stanford University Dr. Philip Zimbardo, the problem with overloading the brain with technology is that it rewires the brain to feel pleasure only when it is being overloaded. Simple pleasures like a sunset begin to fall victim to high-action movies.

Dr. Zimbardo described this as the digital rewiring of the brain. He said that the average video game–playing teenage boy would in essence lose his ability to experience real pleasure in the real world.[14]

God created us for relationship—with him and with others. Excessive media can consume the time and energy we ought to be using to build those relationships. So taking a break from media can help our brains refocus on the things, people, and experiences that provide genuine pleasure—whether that's our spouses, a crackling fire on a cold winter night, or the smell of a fresh, hot pizza straight from the oven. (Man, thinking about that pizza is making me hungry!)

The Elusive Concept of Free Time

What may surprise you most about a media fast is the amount of time that opens up each day—time that can be spent in prayer, Scripture reading, deep conversation, service to others, and slowing down the pace of life.

During my ten days without media, I woke up one morning at 5 a.m. On purpose? Hardly. When you are watching someone else's kids, sometimes you don't have a choice. Normally I see 5 a.m. only if I'm going fishing, hunting, or leaving on vacation. In fact, my first reaction when seeing the clock that early is: "Wow! I forgot there are two 5s in one day." But if the kiddos want to get up at 5, I'll be getting up then too.

I managed to find the energy to get out of bed, and I went downstairs with my buddy CW—the two-year-old responsible for my early awakening—to find something to do. (He and his five-year-old sister were staying with us while his parents enjoyed a much-needed break.) As we got downstairs, it hit me: "I have three hours before I need to be at work!"

Typically I wake up with just enough time for a shower and the drive to work. And on most mornings, I don't even have breakfast until I get to the office around 8 a.m. So having all this downtime wasn't part of my usual routine. Normally downtime is not a problem. By turning on my cell phone, watching an episode of *The Cosby Show,* or checking Facebook, I can fill up any "margin" in my day with stuff. But today I had more than two hours to kill, and I couldn't use any media. What to do?

I began with a made-up stretch routine that felt amazing. Then I actually sat down and ate breakfast without any distractions (other than a two-year-old). Did you know that it's possible to eat breakfast at a table without anything else to do? It was news to me too!

I then unloaded the dishwasher, fed CW, reloaded the dishwasher, played with CW, set the table for breakfast, fixed breakfast for my wife and the rest of the kids, enjoyed a nice leisurely shower, took my time getting ready after my shower, and made it to work on time. Crazy, I know! What a powerful reminder of how much time we can miss in just one day!

Here's an amazing statistic from the same Kaiser study cited earlier: the average American teenager will consume approximately five hours of TV and/or movies per day, and every year those numbers go up.[15] That's just TV and movies, not video games or other media! I fall well short of that number, but that's largely because of the woman I married. "Old Daniel" watched lots of TV and movies—anywhere from fifteen to almost forty hours every week! That's a whole lot of wasted time every day.

But other forms of media still consume much of my day, and my media fast reminded me that I have a lot more free time than I want to admit—it's just a question of how I use that time. I'm confident the same is true for you too.

TIME FOR ACTION

Are you ready to disconnect so you can reconnect with the people who matter most in your life? The action steps for this challenge are much simpler than some of the other experiences in this book. I have just two main recommendations:

Create Your "Fast" List

What media will you abandon and avoid for your ten days? You could get rid of all media distractions, but that probably would require moving to an isolated cabin and cutting off all ties with civilization for ten days. In other words, it just isn't practical. I recommend going to the media journal I mentioned earlier in the chapter. See which types of media are consuming the biggest chunks of your week, and make sure they're on your list to avoid.

Here's the key: chart a course that works for you. This isn't about legalistic adherence to a list of set-in-stone rules. God will still love you if you have to spend time online for your job, and God can still use your sacrifice to draw you closer to him and to other people.

Create Your "Feast" List

I recommend starting your media fast on a weekend. For most of us, there's already more downtime than on a weekday, so it's simpler to spend more time with God and with your family and friends.

Next, prepare to gorge yourself on meaningful relationship time. Get ready to dive into an ocean of quality time with God and with others. Soak up the calmer schedule, and bask in the silence. Intentionally pursue face time and God time during your ten days without media.

A BEAUTIFUL TOOL FOR MAKING CULTURE

If you walk away from this chapter convinced media is inherently evil, then I've failed you. Media is as evil as a brick—it can be constructive or destructive. What you do with it makes it good or bad. Timothy Keller defined art and positive "culture making" as anything that promotes human life and flourishing[16]—which means bad art and culture would take away from and diminish human life and flourishing.

Sometimes the lines are clear, but other times they're fuzzy. Does spending seven-and-a-half hours alone with media promote human life and flourishing? For the most part, I'd say no. Does going to dinner and a movie with your significant other promote human life and flourishing? Probably. Does enjoying a football game with friends promote human life and flourishing? If you're watching the Carolina Panthers, absolutely! (Sorry, sports fans, I had to squeeze in one plug for my favorite team!)

Media can be a beautiful tool for culture making. It can promote human life and flourishing. Technology that allows us to connect with family thousands of miles away can be a great thing. A movie that is challenging and epic, full of rich ideas about family and adventure—that can be a great thing. Inspiring music that helps people cope with the human condition and understand their place in the world—that can be a great thing too. Sadly, much of the media produced in our culture falls short of this ideal.

The problem of excessive media is a global issue. When I was in Romania working with orphans for four months in 2005, a translator told me that most of the children learn Spanish at a relatively young age because they watch so many Spanish soap operas. The good thing about that is they learn a language; the bad thing is that they are exposed to sex-infused programming that is not appropriate for children (or for adults). I also heard on *The Phil Vischer Podcast* that Japan is having a problem getting men to marry and have kids because dating cuts into their time playing video games or on other devices[17]—a negative result.

But even with media's potential for greatness, we all benefit from a break. Our brains need a rest. If we continue consuming media at our current rate, we run the risk of damaging our healthy relationships, decimating our ability to experience pleasure, and never contributing to solving big issues like poverty or human trafficking. Our ability to impact the world, in many ways, could come down to how much media we consume.

Has a fast ever sounded so appealing?

5

Pull Up a Rug

Ten Days Without Furniture to Address Global Poverty

➤ ➤ ➤ If anyone has material possessions and sees his
brother in need but has no pity on him, how
can the love of God be in him?

1 JOHN 3:17

*My name is Daniel Day, and I'm going ten days without furniture
to fight extreme poverty throughout the world. For the next ten
days I will not be using any furniture. Ten days. No furniture. Starts
now.*

Day 9…I've heard it said that lying on the floor is good
for your posture. If that's true, I should have amazing
posture by the time I'm done tomorrow night! Evidently
my back and neck have needed a lot of correcting
because they've been sore for the past nine days. Every
once in a while my wife's arm falls off the side of the bed
as she's sleeping comfortably on a luscious pillow-top

mattress; it's like she's taunting me. Meanwhile, my shoulders are struggling to dig deep enough into the carpet to relax my neck. Despite the discomfort, ten days without furniture has been a great experience where I've learned to appreciate what I have. But I'm excited about drawing this thing to a close.

As a side note, I've also heard the urban legend that says the average human swallows between seven to twelve spiders while sleeping each year. Even though it's not true, I still wonder how many bugs I've swallowed while sleeping on the floor over the past nine days. Last night, I even dreamed that an earthworm crawled into my mouth. In the dream, I spit it out, but couldn't get rid of the worm's grainy dirt taste. When I finally woke up to the sound of our three-month-old not sleeping, it was the first time I was thankful to be awake in the middle of the night.

Regardless of the discomfort and dreams, it's amazing to be a part of this calling to make a real difference in the world. I know that going without furniture doesn't really sound like a big deal, and in the grand scheme of things ten days is nothing. But doing these challenges, and going without these "necessities," has really reminded me of how blessed I am for things like shoes and a bed. It's brought back into focus how out-of-whack my life is compared with the majority of the world.

GLOBALLY SPEAKING, WE ARE NOT POOR

If you bought this book, you are not poor. If deciding what clothes to wear each day takes longer than thirty seconds, you are not poor. If you regularly eat at sit-down restaurants, you are not poor. If you visit the mall and sometimes return home with bags from one or two or ten stores, you are not poor. If you see movies at the movie theater (not counting the dollar movie theater), you are not poor.

Many of us *feel* poor at times (especially if you're a teenager or in your early twenties). But our feelings of "poverty" usually surface when we compare ourselves to other people. *Our neighbors have a new car. Our friends moved into a huge house. Her wardrobe seems like it walked right off a runway in Paris. He always has the latest tech gadgets.* We buy into the culture's lies about what we *should* own and how we *should* live.

Yes, we've gone through tough times recently in our nation's economy (and the global economy), and maybe you and your family have struggled. And yes, many people in Western nations have real problems with poverty and need our help. We cannot ignore them by sending our help and support only to the developing world.

But in general there is a difference between the way we struggle and the way people struggle in the developing world. Ever missed a meal because you didn't have money to buy rice and beans at the grocery store? Can you fit all your clothes into a small backpack? Have you gone an entire winter without heat at home?

Friends, we are not poor.

Changing Our Perspective

A few years ago, my wife and I ran out of money. It's the closest we've come to experiencing true poverty. We were in between jobs and trying to fund-raise for our next opportunity. Rebecca and I had decided to join a new ministry a couple of months before, and we were still waiting for God to bring in the money we needed to start our work. One night, I couldn't sleep because of stress. I'd been consumed with worry about finances, and I was discouraged because it felt like we could never get ahead. I was frustrated with God, frustrated with our circumstances, and frustrated with—well, everything!

As I sat on the couch, my heart filled with anxiety, an idea came into my head: *What if Rebecca and I walked through the house and thanked God for everything that we had?*

At the time, we lived in a townhome with a long floor plan that almost felt like a houseboat (without the rolling waves that can leave me seasick, of course). My idea was to start in the living room and pray as we slowly walked through each room. Rebecca went along with my weird plan, even though her expression seemed to suggest, "I'm glad no one else can see us right now!"

We started praying at the front of the house:

God, thank you for a house that keeps us warm during the winter and cool during the summer. Thank you for blinds that keep our neighbors from staring at us when we are sitting on the couch. Thank you for our TV, the bookshelves full of books, decorations above our couch,

curtains to decorate the windows, a couch, a sofa table, a
dining room table, chairs to sit at the table, a china cabinet
to hold decorations for the dining room, a garage to store
our car, a car to get us where we need to go, woodworking
tools to build things, two bicycles, a kitchen with a fridge,
a stove, an oven, a microwave, food in the fridge, cabinets
to hold pots and pans and plates and cups, a sink, a trash
can, a closet full of random unopened boxes from when
we moved in, everything in the random unopened boxes,
a shower curtain, a toilet, a sink, running water, hot water,
electricity, a crib, baby toys…

By the time we'd made it halfway through the house, I was
annoyed—not at God but at myself! We had so much stuff that
it was overwhelming, and I couldn't help but apologize to God for
even suggesting that we were poor and impoverished. I almost
packed our car full of stuff for a trip to Goodwill the next day!

More, More, More!

In a marketing culture where nothing is neutral and thousands of
ads each day try to sell us stuff, we easily can believe the lie that
we lack important things. If we have one car or rent a house or
apartment, that means we are poor and in need. And even if we
get the second car or buy a nice house, that's still not enough. We
are told daily that we need more and more and *more*! It's enough
to make us constantly struggle with coveting—wanting something that's not ours. Every day we see something that we don't

have, something that we want. The marketing messages work because they distract us from a profound reality: compared to most of the world, we are rich.

But after praying through our little townhome that night and realizing how much my wife and I actually had, I felt privileged and wealthy and blessed—and humbled that I so easily take it all for granted.

Have you ever prayed that kind of prayer?

Stop reading for a moment, and spend five minutes walking around and offering a prayer of thanks to God. Thank God for everything in your home and your life—yes, even the knit sweater your grandma gave you last Christmas or the mismatched furniture in your living room or the huge box of ramen noodles in the cupboard. This is a powerful experience, especially if you've found yourself feeling "poor" or thinking your life is "missing" good stuff.

Abandoning the Comforts of Furniture

All of this first-world privilege and wealth made it tough for me to grasp what it would be like to survive on just two dollars a day, like so many people on this planet do. According to the World Bank Group, "1.2 billion people remain below the extreme poverty line with an income of US $1.25 or less a day. In all, 2.4 billion live on less than US $2 a day."[18]

It didn't compute in my brain. I spend more than that anytime I shop at, well, anywhere! That's why I needed to do something extreme, something that could help me get a stronger taste of poverty and remember all the blessings that I have. And going without furniture seemed like one of the most memorable, experiential ways to do that.

Did you know that the average American household has four beds, seven chairs, three couches, and four tables? Okay, I made up those statistics. I don't actually know if those numbers are accurate, but it sure sounds like it! Our beds, our couches, our chairs, our desks—we take them all for granted. We feel entitled to them. They're evidence of our cultural excess and our tendency to take God's blessings for granted.

Someone once asked me if going without furniture really meant going without *all* furniture. There had to be some kind of exception, right? You can use a bed, can't you? Or you get one chair, don't you? (Because of the timing of my challenge, I did make an exception—more about that near the end of the chapter.) I assured my friend that going without furniture truly meant I would go without furniture. No bed. No chairs. No tables. No desk. (It didn't mean I would pull all my clothes from my dresser, though!)

I knew that going without a bed would be tough. It's where we all spend eight hours of each day. (Well, doctors say that's how long we should sleep. I'm more of a seven-and-a-half-hours-per-night kinda guy, but I digress.) It's where we relax at the end of a long, tiring day. When you wake up from a good night of sleep, you feel refreshed and ready to tackle the new day.

Sleeping on the floor? Yup, it was as rough as I imagined it would be.

But I also encountered lots of other little moments during

the day when I missed furniture. My chair and desk at the office. My table and chair at dinnertime. I spent a lot of time standing—and sitting on the floor.

We Really Can Make a Difference

Here's what I learned: God opens our eyes in all kinds of ways—even through a sore body! Pain can make us aware. Discomfort can motivate us to act. A body that's sore will get better, but people living on two bucks a day face an uncertain future. They might have no heat for the winter, beyond what a fire can create. They might wear clothes until the fabric truly, literally falls apart. They might go to bed hungry because the cupboard is bare.

My heartbreak grew with each day as I considered the conditions under which so many people live in the world—and even in some places in developed countries like the United States. I realized that any money I could raise would make a big difference to those who'd receive help.

The problem of poverty is real, and it's devastating. But we can do something about it. There are ways we can help families get out of extreme poverty.

According to Dr. Scott Todd, renowned expert on global poverty and senior vice president of International Partner Development for Compassion International, we can eradicate extreme poverty by the year 2035. Dr. Todd explained that as recently as 1981, 52 percent of the world lived in extreme poverty. But due to technological advances, along with such efforts as providing clean water and vaccines for preventable diseases, the percentage of those living in extreme poverty has now dropped to 26 percent.[19]

How do we reduce this number to zero? We must make some sacrifices and choose to live for something bigger than ourselves. No, we don't need to get rid of all our furniture. But we can do something. We can put our faith into action and share God's love and hope in tangible ways. Ten Days Without is a great place to start.

THE FACE OF GLOBAL POVERTY

If you spend time on social media, you're likely familiar with the hashtag #FirstWorldProblems—a shortcut way of noting that a person's complaints or observations aren't truly significant in the global scheme of things. "I hate when I have to charge my phone twice in one day #FirstWorldProblems." "Gotta stop visiting all-you-can-eat buffet places; leave feeling sick from all the food #FirstWorldProblems." "We don't have room in the garage for my snowboard anymore #FirstWorldProblems."

You get the idea.

But the problem of global poverty is nothing to laugh about. About 780 million people live in extreme poverty and don't have access to essential things such as clean drinking water, food, and shelter. Many of those are children who get caught in extreme poverty and end up dropping out of school to help their families.[20]

Those statistics came to life when I traveled with Compassion International to Honduras in 2012. I wanted to learn about poverty and see how Compassion released children from poverty in Jesus's name. I could visualize the poor based on the many documentaries and photos I had seen growing up. But none of this prepared me for the experience of witnessing what it actually looks like to have *nothing*.

Hope for a Better Life

I was stunned when I saw where people lived. Some houses were made out of concrete, others from mud and sticks. We visited a family that lived in a small building made of concrete blocks, coated in a thin layer of concrete, and topped with a metal roof. A big crack ran down the side of the house. Small wooden posts held up the covering over the porch, which also served as the kitchen. A wood-burning mud stove was just off the porch, and next to it sat a chipped plastic container, mostly full of greenish water. A decrepit container of water was the closest thing to indoor plumbing you could find in the small village.

Beyond the mud stove was a cloth structure with walls made of five wooden posts connected by ripped sheets and old clothes. I glanced through the opening and noticed a white five-gallon bucket in the center of the small structure. This was the outhouse.

I walked up to the porch, and the family welcomed our group inside to see their home. It felt awkward, but curiosity got the best of me and I stuck my head through the door. The house had one room and one window. The concrete floor was nicely swept, and a broom of dried weeds gathered together with twine and tied to a stick sat in the corner. The family owned two pieces of furniture: a small side table with a full jar of beans atop its rough, handmade surface and a twin-size bed covered with one sheet. The bed sagged in the middle, and that's when I noticed a little boy sitting where a pillow would normally go against the cold concrete wall.

Slowly, as our team talked with the father, the family's story became clearer. The father was a farmer, and his family of four rented the home from another family member. All four of them—dad, mom, son, and daughter—slept on that one bed. Our group leader asked him about the church program his children participated in. (Most locals do not know that Compassion is responsible for helping their kids. Compassion does everything through the local church, so that people see the church as the source of the help and support. After all, that's what it is.)

"What do you like most about the program?" the leader asked.

The dad paused for a moment, while his small children clung to his legs. His son and daughter were wearing bright-colored shirts that they had received from the church.

"Hope," the father responded in a quiet, reserved voice. "I don't want my kids to have this life. I've always wanted them to have a better one but never thought it was possible. The program gives me hope that they can and will have a better life."

It was obvious from the dad's voice that he had given up on his own ability to get out of poverty. But instead of being discouraged by his future, he had a twinkle of optimism in his eye. He could still be successful if his kids were able to escape extreme poverty.

A Place Called Home

At another house in Honduras, a single father was raising two boys (one of the boys was the child I mentioned in chapter 2, whose life was saved through the Compassion-sponsored medical program). Instead of concrete blocks, their home was made from baked mud and sticks, and instead of a nice concrete floor, they had dirt. No wonder hurricanes do so much damage to places like that, because there's no way that construction could retain the metal roof through harsh winds.

Inside his house, he had used cardboard and lashing to split one room into two. Ironically, the cardboard was the box from someone's brand-new LCD TV. One man's trash is another man's interior wall.

I was literally standing in extreme poverty. It was hot, sweaty, dirty, and smelly. Standing inside that hut in Honduras was the first time the reality of poverty was clear to me.

I have seen numerous commercials on TV about poor children, I have watched quite a few documentaries, and I have received plenty of mail asking me to help fight poverty. But it took seeing it in person—seeing the squalor in which people live every single day—for me to feel the need. These encounters gave me a greater appreciation for the roof over my head, the bed and furniture under my body, and the carpet under my feet.

STORIES FROM OTHER ADVENTURERS

Going ten days without furniture isn't something that you do halfheartedly. This challenge is tough, and if you undertake it, you will experience some pain. (Not trying to discourage you, but I also don't want you to think it's gonna be easy!) You may not want to hear this, but the physical, emotional, or mental pain is an important part of the experience because the discomfort can help you recognize and appreciate all your blessings.

Not surprisingly, people who have gone without furniture often share this comment: they didn't sleep well.

Katy, a teenager from the Midwest, e-mailed me what she had recorded in her journal after doing this challenge. She said after day one:

> So last night [was awful]! I got maybe four hours of sleep
> and woke up with the worst headache ever.

Feeling even worse by day three, she wrote this in her journal:

> I'm really feeling the pain in my lower back today. I def-
> initely got more sleep last night than the night before, but
> I think it's because I took one of my sweatshirts and used it
> as a pillow. I'm not feeling quite as blessed today, I think
> the lack of rest and the pain is kind of going to my head,
> which might explain the headaches I've been having.

The challenge didn't just affect her sleep. Even work was a challenge:

> Work today was really difficult for me; I couldn't sit down
> for break and there was no way I was going to sit on the
> dirty floor, so I leaned against a wall—which means I
> stood for a good six hours [straight].

You totally feel God leading you to skip this challenge, don't you? Just kidding—but I do want you to be prepared for the difficulty of going without furniture. But even though it's uncomfortable, the discomfort of going ten days without furniture helps us care more about people whose lives are defined by true, abject poverty. Katy put it this way:

> I've definitely come to realize that what I'm doing with this fasting/challenge is much more than just sitting on the ground and blogging about my daily experience. It makes me really think about those who are constantly on the cold ground or those who have never truly been comfortable. God has blessed us so much with everything we have. Most of what we use in our daily lives we take for granted. But to those who have nothing, who have never slept in a bed or sat on a couch, or even snuggled with a pillow, this stuff would mean the world to them to just experience it, let alone to claim it as their own.… I really believe Ten Days Without Furniture focuses me toward those who have never felt comfort in their lives or maybe don't even know what comfort is.… For ten days I am uncomfortable for those who are broken in their lack of comfort.

Going without furniture—or any of the other challenges you might take on—is more than personal experience and blogging. It's about making a difference in the world. It's about the sacrifice and pain that lead you to a better understanding of an important issue and what you can do about it. God used Ten Days Without Furniture to remind Katy of how good her life is, and I believe God can do that for you too.

You Have a Lot to Give

But what if you don't feel like you can raise much money to donate? What if you are young and don't believe you have the resources or ability to fight an issue as overwhelming as poverty? What if you give all the donations you collect and it still feels like *nothing*?

I understand that feeling. But an encounter with an elementary school–aged Honduran girl named Crisvin changed my perspective.

When I met Crisvin, I had just spent an hour playing soccer with a bunch of kids under the hot Honduran sun. I looked rough and flushed, smelled bad, and was chugging water from a water bottle—exactly the way we all want to make a first impression! But that didn't keep Crisvin from giving me the biggest hug ever. She was beautiful. She had olive skin, black hair pulled back into a ponytail, timid eyes above cheeks full of dimples, and was wearing a light green checkered dress.

Soon it was time to get on the bus with some of the children in the Compassion program, tour the village, and take the kids and their family members to their homes. One of the stops was at Crisvin's home. Crisvin sat next to me on the bus, and her aunt, who was taking care of her that day, sat in front of us. I took the opportunity to ask Crisvin's aunt about Crisvin and her family. Her dad had abandoned the family, and her mom worked in a city several hours away from the home. Her grandmother and aunt did their best to help fill the void.

"Does Crisvin's mom make enough to provide for them?" I asked her aunt, who was responsible for bringing her to Compassion's program.

"Not right now. She has only been at the job for a couple of weeks and is still training. The workers at the factory get paid for each parachute they stuff. Right now Crisvin's mom is making two dollars a day. Some of the ladies that she works with have been there a lot longer, and they can stuff enough parachutes to make fifty dollars a week. Crisvin's mom will get there soon; she is a hard worker."

There it was: someone who actually made two dollars a day. Crisvin's mom was responsible for taking care of herself, a daughter, a son, and Crisvin's grandma on two dollars a day. She wasn't a statistic; she was a real-life person who worked an entire day but earned less than what I spend each time I go inside a coffee shop or burger joint.

An Unexpected Gift

The family's house was made from green wood paneling and had a concrete floor. It was a one-room shack the size of the master bathroom in my house. Inside, the family's limited possessions were quite organized. The shelves were tightly packed with odds and ends, and the concrete floor was swept perfectly. The walls were covered with pictures of their family, and I noticed all of Crisvin's diplomas from passing different grades in school.

Their family was blessed to have two small twin beds that

were pushed together. Grandma, mom, Crisvin, and her younger brother slept on those two beds. Crisvin's bed was covered with a Barbie blanket that was tucked in neatly on all sides. She pulled out two dolls, and we sat on her bed and played with them for a few minutes.

When our team leader said it was time to go, I grabbed Crisvin and held her in a big bear hug. I knew a little bit of Spanish and used every bit of it to tell her that she was beautiful, that I loved her, and that I would write to her soon. She was my new pen pal, and I couldn't wait to get back and send her a letter.

As I let her go, she reached into the small backpack that held all her toys and pulled out a small wooden container. She opened the lid, dumped out her dolls' shoes and accessories on the bed, and then handed the round wooden box to me.

"This is for you," she said.

"For me? Crisvin, I can't take this," I replied.

"I want you to have it because you are my family."

"Thank you!" I said and pulled her close for one more hug. My heart was overwhelmed. I have never experienced a more difficult dilemma in my life than whether or not I should accept that gift. How could I take something from a little girl who has so little?

Giving Beyond Your Ability

A few months later, Crisvin's small gift made more sense as I was reading part of a letter that Paul sent to the Corinthians. He was talking about the Macedonians, describing their generosity: "And now, brothers, we want you to know about the grace that God has given the Macedonian churches. Out of the most severe trial, their overflowing joy and their extreme poverty welled up in rich generosity. For I testify that they gave as much as they were able, and even beyond their ability. Entirely on their own" (2 Corinthians 8:1–3). Later Paul told the Corinthians that if they were cheerful givers, they would "be made rich in every way so that you can be generous on every occasion, and through us your generosity will result in thanksgiving to God" (2 Corinthians 9:11).

That day in Honduras, Crisvin gave as much as she was able to a guy who didn't need it, and that small gift resulted in thanksgiving to God. As a comparatively rich American, I struggle with giving, yet she gave out of her poverty. Crisvin was a modern-day version of the widow with two copper coins who, Jesus said, "put more into the treasury than all the others. They all gave out of their wealth; but she, out of her poverty, put in everything—all she had to live on" (Mark 12:43–44).

Crisvin, a victim of poverty, owned a small, round wooden box for her dolls' accessories. She could have said, "I don't have anything to give," but she didn't. That small wooden box sits on my desk next to my new computer, smartphone, and coffee mug to remind me that generosity is not determined by the amount we give but by the sacrifice that a gift requires.

You may think that you don't have much to offer because you are too young. You may think that you don't have enough money to combat a large problem like poverty. But you have a lot to offer, even if it doesn't seem like a lot to you. God knows your attitude and the condition of your heart. We all have something to give; a young girl from Honduras and going ten days without furniture helped me remember that.

TIME FOR ACTION

Going without furniture is one of the most jarring adventures you'll ever embark on. It will rock your daily routines and create a powerful awareness of the blessings in your life. But remember that the goal is to do more than just feel and experience things for yourself—you have the opportunity to raise awareness, gather donations, and engage other people in addressing global poverty. Here are some essential steps to follow:

Choose a Strategy That Matters to You

Adopt the strategy that resonates with you most strongly. You could do a campaign to get children sponsored, or you could do a fund-raiser for an organization that addresses a particular aspect of poverty. I prefer sponsoring a child because you get the benefits of writing letters and building a relationship with that child, but both strategies can make a difference.

Find the Best Partner

Choose an organization that you can believe in. If your church has a ministry to the needy or partnerships with mission groups around the world, that can be a great place for your donations. Different charities and organizations address various aspects of fighting poverty through a wide range of programs, such as child sponsorship, food and relief, building wells to provide clean water, farming and advanced agricultural techniques, designing schools or churches, and several others. If you need assistance with finding a partner organization or setting up a fund-raiser or child-sponsorship campaign, go to 10dayswithout.com and click on "Partner Organizations" or "Start a Campaign."

Inform and Involve People

Tell people what you are doing—and why you're doing it. Share it on all of your social media pages, send out e-mails or letters, and explain how people can get involved in the cause. Print cards to hand out to curious observers who want to know more. (See the 10dayswithout.com website for templates. Click on "Promo Material.")

Share the Details

Use your blog (or submit your posting to 10dayswithout.com) and other social media to talk about your adventures. What unexpected lessons are you learning? Where is it most difficult to go without furniture? How does your back feel each morning? And wherever possible, tie it all back to the problem of global poverty, and tell people how they can make a difference.

Doing the challenge, sharing your experiences, and raising money for your sponsored organization will help you do your part to reduce poverty in the world.

LESSONS FROM A WEDDING

A final thought for you to chew on: be prepared for God to teach you some unexpected lessons during these challenges—something that happened to me when I went without furniture.

Blame my horrible timing or a calendar malfunction for this one, but I didn't realize that my furniture-free time would overlap my sister's wedding. And a week before the big day, my sister needed to meet with the florist to finalize some details, so I decided to go along. You can see where this is going, right?

The eclectic flower shop in the small town of Hendersonville, North Carolina, smelled amazing—almost overwhelming. I felt as if I'd opened up a giant jar of potpourri and had jumped inside. (I wonder how many times *that* YouTube video would be watched.) Once we met the florist, she offered me a seat, which meant I had to explain why I wasn't using furniture. She and her assistant both laughed awkwardly, and for the first time during a challenge, I felt silly. They tried to get back to the wedding details, but the sight of me sitting on the floor next to an unoccupied chair was too rich to leave alone. The florist and her assistant kept coming back to my experiment with some humorous statement or question.

"What are you going to do at the reception—will you sit at the table?"

"How are you going to cut a filet if you're holding your plate?"

"It's a good thing you didn't do Ten Days Without Shoes during the wedding. Bare feet would have ruined the pictures!"

I quickly realized my sister's wedding was playing second fiddle to my sitting on the floor. And that's when I reached an important conclusion: sometimes our good intentions, our desire to help, and our commitment to a cause can actually take away from others. Inspiring people to help fight poverty is a very noble cause, but I didn't want to take away from my sister's big day.

So I created an exception to Ten Days Without. I decided to use furniture and not draw any attention to myself during the wedding or reception. The principle buried in that exception became an important characteristic of all the experiments moving forward. I would be careful to honor other people above perfectly following the rules of the experiment.

As you get involved in these challenges, remember my example. Remember that love is more important than earning a perfect score during your ten days without. (Seriously, no one will grade you. This isn't a research project for some cantankerous English teacher.) Remember that the way you do the challenge is just as important as the result. A cause is a great thing to live for, but we defeat the purpose if we hurt the people we love.

6

Life Without Limitations

Ten Days Without Legs to Address Our Response to Disabilities

➤ ➤ ➤ Then he turned to his host. "When you put on a luncheon or a banquet," he said, "don't invite your friends, brothers, relatives, and rich neighbors. For they will invite you back, and that will be your only reward. Instead, invite the poor, the crippled, the lame, and the blind. Then at the resurrection of the righteous, God will reward you for inviting those who could not repay you."

LUKE 14:12–14, NLT

My name is Daniel Day, and I'm going ten days without using my legs to raise money and recruit volunteers to help people affected by disabilities. I will use a wheelchair to get around. I will be driven to work and dropped off at home by family and friends. I will not stand in the shower or walk up stairs. Ten days. No legs. Starts now.

Day 1…I'm sitting at the kitchen table in my wheelchair.
So far this morning, I took a shower, dressed myself,

climbed down thirteen stairs with only my arms, and already I feel like it's been a full day. Normally it would take around thirty minutes to do my morning routine, but I'm already pushing an hour.

Lesson Number 1: Plan on everything taking at least twice as long for the next ten days.

It only took me about three minutes to figure out that my entire life caters to standing up and walking. We have a wooden medicine cabinet in our bathroom above the sink—my deodorant, razor, and shaving cream are all too high for me to reach. Then there's the design of our rental house as a whole: stairs, a raised entryway, and soft carpet. I can't imagine what a family goes through when they find out Dad had an accident at work and is paralyzed from the waist down or that Mom lost her legs while serving in Afghanistan. I guess they have to sell their house or put it through some major renovations.

Biggest challenge today? Putting pants on by myself. First, I tried sitting on the edge of my bed with my legs hanging limply below me. Every time I tried to reach down with my hand and pull up one of my legs to slide it into a leg hole, I almost fell off the bed on my face. Then I tried lying down, but couldn't pull up my pants success-fully without subconsciously using my leg muscles. Not wanting to cheat, I had to abandon that strategy. Finally, I found that sitting on the floor and leaning on the opposite arm from the leg I was trying to clothe was successful, and after ten minutes of trying, I had pants on.

What was my wife doing this entire time? Standing there, pointing at me, and laughing. At least I gave her ten minutes of humor to start her day.

AUTHENTIC COMMUNITY

You find out who your friends are when you end up in a wheelchair. It was amazing to see people step up and lend a hand. It was one of the few times in my life when I actually experienced genuine Christian community—the kind that's made of sacrifice, compassion, service, and most importantly love.

Rebecca had to take me to work. My boss, Jeremiah, brought me home from work. My coworker Nicholas had to carry me up two flights of stairs while a different coworker, Daniel, had to carry my wheelchair. People had to drive me places, get me things, and make sacrifices for me.

And although it was a burden on everyone, a few people told me it was their favorite of my Ten Days Without challenges. Nicholas said it was great because it required other people to help. And I think I agree with him. As Christians, we need to live life more vulnerably. We need to admit it when we need help and to help when we are needed. Ten Days Without Legs taught me some valuable truths about the role of community and reminded me that we need it a lot more than we think we do.

And the whole experience taught me to be aware of people with disabilities. We see them almost every day, represented in a person at the store, at school, or in our own families. But we don't always know how to interact with them. We don't want the other person to feel awkward, but that ends up making us feel awkward about whether either of us feels awkward. (Remind you of a bunch of seventh graders at a junior high dance?)

I decided to go ten days without using my legs so that I could understand the world of disability a little better and as a way to educate others on how they can help. I also did it because I like a challenge and thought a lot of people would read my blog because they wanted to see me suffer—but that's less spiritual and perhaps a little too honest, so let's focus on the "helping" part.

An Opportunity to Serve

I first became aware of the rewards of serving and helping people with disabilities back in high school. A Sunday school class at our church had a few children with disabilities, and the teacher was looking for volunteers to come in once a week and play with a child affected by Down syndrome for two hours, while his parents enjoyed a break and went to the main service.

As a sixteen-year-old, I was nervous about interacting with Corey, the child affected by Down syndrome. I didn't know what to do, what to say, or how to handle him. But the Sunday school teacher was patient with me and kept telling me one simple thing: "Just play with him, Daniel. That's all Corey wants. He just wants you to play with him."

So that's what we did. We built block towers, ate crackers, and read books. We also occasionally crashed block towers, spilled crackers, and ripped books. I loved those two hours every week, and Corey responded so well to our time together.

A Long-Awaited Reunion

Years later, after I had graduated from college and was working full time, I volunteered at a Special Olympics event in town. It was held at the local high school and was the biggest Special Olympics in that part of the state. I was responsible for a game tent, where athletes affected by disabilities could come and hang out between their races.

It was an amazing day. I interacted with hundreds of people—and ate way too much cotton candy. (Amazing how food makes certain events particularly memorable.) But the best part of the day was when I looked up and saw a much older Corey barreling toward me with the biggest smile on his face, yelling my name. I could barely brace myself before he jumped into my arms and gave me a bear hug. A kid who shouldn't have recognized me, much less remembered my name. Up to that point in my life, I had never felt that important.

If you ever doubt your ability to make a difference in the life and family of someone affected by a disability, remember the story of Corey. You don't have to invest a lot of time, and you don't have to adopt a child with Down syndrome—although either of those would be an amazing thing to do. Making a difference in the world of disabilities simply means caring enough to learn and then using your knowledge to show a person affected by disability, in the best way possible, that you love him or her.

AWARENESS AND INVOLVEMENT

The goal of Ten Days Without Legs was not to do a fund-raiser or collect items of clothing. Instead, I identified two goals: recruit volunteers for the organization I was sponsoring—Joni and Friends, a ministry started by Joni Eareckson Tada to serve people with disabilities and their families—and educate people about how to interact with those affected by disabilities. I don't actually know how many people read my blog and then found places to serve in their communities. Because this was one of my earliest challenges, I wasn't thinking about tracking the effectiveness.

But I do know that this experience had a huge impact on my heart, and I know that quite a few people were challenged by the information they read about disabilities; so that alone makes it worth the sacrifice.

As you consider doing this challenge yourself, know that you will gain a much deeper understanding of disabilities, but you can also educate others about how they can help and recruit volunteers for worthwhile organizations and ministries. It's okay if you don't know how many people volunteer because of your experiment— as long as you can see the life change that takes place in you and pass on to others a better understanding of people with disabilities.

Physically Demanding Experience
That being said, going ten days without using my legs was the most physically demanding challenge I have ever attempted! I

used my arms to do everything, including climbing stairs, getting in and out of the car, and propelling my wheelchair. (Go to 10day swithout.com to see the video of me using my arms to climb the stairs.) No other part of my body was more eager for this segment to be finished, especially because navigating a wheelchair is not as easy as it looks.

But Ten Days Without Legs was also incredibly inconvenient. My wife explained this really well:

> I have to admit, for a wife that helped come up with the idea of Ten Days Without, I was not excited about this experiment. Sure, everyone else was rooting for Daniel to do Ten Days Without Legs, but they are not the ones living with him. I did my fair share of grumbling this week. Every morning I had to wake up and get two little boys in the car and get their daddy to work on time (not that we were actually on time once this week). I tried my best to coerce my husband to drive himself, but in the end driving our car is something that takes legs, so he refused.
>
> A little flustered from our quick departure, I would pull up to the office, hop out and get Daniel's heavy wheelchair from the trunk. He would "drop" into his chair, load up his lap with work stuff, and off he went. That's when it would hit me: he really could be in a wheelchair. Seeing my husband roll off was humbling. How on earth could I be complaining; we only have to do this for ten days not a lifetime. I am so blessed.

Rebecca alludes to the most humbling part of this experiment: I couldn't do it on my own. Most of the other Ten Days Without challenges were sacrifices that I could endure on my own—but Ten Days Without Legs required everyone in my life to help out.

Life with a Disability

And that's the daily reality for the millions of people around the globe who are affected by disabilities. According to disabled world.com, 10 percent of the world's population, or roughly 650 million people, live with disabilities.[21] And sadly, people with disabilities in developing countries have a really hard time finding help. Wheelchairs often are either unaffordable or nonexistent, and there is also a lack of expert medical and educational support for families in the developing world.

Think about it. Here in the United States we have special classes for people with special needs. We have researchers and hospitals with teams devoted to mental health and supporting affected families. Those resources don't exist in much of the world.

Of course, that doesn't mean it's a cakewalk for families in the United States to cope with disabilities—it's difficult anywhere. But there are great opportunities to serve individuals in the developing world because of the tremendous need.

Maybe serving internationally stirs up your passion. If so, a great place to start is the Joni and Friends Wheels for the World ministry program. This ministry collects donated wheelchairs, repairs them, and distributes them to people in developing nations.

The program also distributes Bibles and shares the message of Jesus with people receiving the wheelchairs. But I didn't want to do an international trip. I wanted to find people in the United States I could serve. I will tell you more about that later.

Different Kinds of Disabilities

It's also important to realize the wide range of disabilities. We make a mistake if we group everyone with a disability into the same category. People are affected by a lot of different kinds of disabilities and can be affected to different degrees and different levels of severity. Each person also has a unique set of needs. It's important for us to learn as much as we can about disabilities in general so that we can identify what people really need help with—and then help them.

Physical disabilities affect mobility, motion, and motor skills. Some of these struggles happen as a result of genetics, and some occur as a result of an accident or crime. Later in this chapter I'll tell you about my experiences at a Joni and Friends Family Retreat. While there, I was responsible for Bryce, who used a wheelchair because of a birth defect and was paralyzed from the waist down. And at the retreat I also met John, who was in a wheelchair—not because of the way he was born but because of an accident. Both are examples of physical disability. Physical disability can also include people who have a visual impairment such as blindness.

The category of intellectual and developmental disabilities (IDDs) includes autism, Down syndrome, and many others. Most of these disabilities cause a disconnect between an individual and what is considered age-appropriate ability and behavior. Just as physical disabilities have a range of severity, IDDs have a range as well. For example, there is a major difference between someone with slight autism and someone with severe autism. Someone with slight autism may not be able to understand a sarcastic joke; someone with a severe case of autism may be completely unable to use any kind of spoken language.

God calls us to help others, to carry one another's burdens, and to do whatever we can to love people. When we serve people living with disabilities, it's important to be aware and informed—just as we ought to be compassionate and loving.

OREGON: THE FAMILY RETREAT

Going ten days without legs was difficult, and I gained a much better understanding of what it's like to have a mobile disability. But for me, it wasn't enough. I knew that if I was going to understand the world of disabilities, I needed something more.

While talking with some of the staff at Joni and Friends, I found out about their family retreats. It seemed like the perfect setting to learn about disabilities, and as a bonus I would get to serve a family. Joni and Friends offers family retreats all across the United States, but by the time I discovered them, it was already late into the summer. If I was going to attend, I needed to fly to Oregon for a retreat that would be held right on the Pacific Ocean.

Yes, I was willing to make that sacrifice!

Oregon in the summer is beautiful. The grass is green, the

trees are lush, and the temperature is just right. As I drove through Tillamook State Forest, I had a hard time keeping my eyes on the road. The giant trees were covered with moss, and the road wound alongside a beautiful and wide river, sparkling in the afternoon sunlight. I kept thinking how I'd like to come back here and do some fly-fishing.

Wisdom Along the Road

I wasn't making the trip alone; in fact, I wasn't even driving my car. A sweet elderly woman named Caroline had picked me up from the Portland International Airport, and after traveling all day from Arizona, she hoped that I would be willing to drive to the retreat site. I was willing and followed her directions out of the city and onto the long road that led through the forest toward the ocean.

Caroline was passionate about this particular retreat, having served there for years and accumulated a wealth of knowledge. We spent a lot of the two-hour trip discussing what I should expect.

"You will love this retreat, Daniel," she said with her tender and experienced voice. "This is one of my favorite weeks of the year."

"What makes it so special?" I asked.

"There is nothing more difficult and physically demanding than taking care of some of these kids. There is also nothing as rewarding. Every night I fall into bed exhausted, and yet I can't wait to wake up the next day and serve again. There is nothing like completely depleting your energy to help another human being. Every time I leave here, I can't wait to come back."

Serving and Caring for Families

Caroline explained that we would be serving as short-term mission-aries (STM is the way Joni and Friends refers to the role) and we would each come alongside someone affected by some sort of dis-ability—essentially, be the person's helper and friend for the week.

"But don't they have people who take care of them already?" I asked.

"Most of them have excellent parents and caretakers. But those parents and caretakers never get a break during the year—we give them a much-needed break."

Joni and Friends Family Retreats are times of renewal for families affected by disability. Parents of a son or daughter af-fected by autism, Down syndrome, or some other disability have a much more difficult home life than most other families. They face more financial burdens, more stress in their marriages (in-cluding a high divorce rate), and almost never have time for themselves.

Siblings have a hard time as well. They often find themselves in parenting roles with more responsibilities than other kids their age. They often feel neglected, not as important, and alone—their friends don't understand what they have to deal with.

"I always work with a girl named Katy," Caroline told me. "She has some very substantial disabilities and can be quite a handful. Last year, her mom came up to me during the retreat and told me, 'Caroline, I'm *so* happy! I got to take a shower and do my makeup and hair—alone!' The family retreat was the first time she could remember being able to bathe in quiet—without being in a hurry—because she didn't have to worry about her daughter.

Can you imagine being a mom of a special-needs daughter and never having a moment to yourself?"

"I can't imagine being a mom!" I joked. "But yeah, I see what you mean. So we are the ones who take care of the son or daughter or brother or sister for the week, while the parents and siblings get some rest?"

"Exactly. The parents and siblings also get spiritual and emotional rest and encouragement. That is just as important as taking a shower and getting a chance to do their makeup!"

"Very cool."

Preparing for a Week of Service

A few hours later, we arrived at the beautiful retreat center situated right next to the Pacific Ocean. I unloaded my bags into my room and helped Caroline get her bags to her room. I decided to get a good night's sleep, so I went to bed early. If what Caroline said was true, I was going to need as much rest as I could get.

After breakfast the next day, we began training for the week. The family retreat couldn't operate without volunteers. Volunteers set up activities, serve food, fill the role of STMs, and complete a plethora of other tasks.

Day one of training went well, and I learned a lot. Rachel, who was responsible for training, had a son who was disabled. She spoke not only as an expert but also as a parent. Her son Bryce had a pair of disabilities. He was born with spina bifida, a birth defect where the spine is located outside the infant's back. This resulted in him being paralyzed from the waist down. Rachel taught us how to assist someone in a wheelchair by using her son as the example—Bryce was the example for a lot of things that week. He was also the camper I ended up working with.

At noon the next day, we prepared to welcome families. Our job was to be as loud and as excited as possible—that wasn't a problem!

Building a New Friendship

Bryce was the first camper to "arrive"—even though he had already been at the retreat center for two days, he still loved going through the entryway and watching everyone get excited. It was a little awkward acting excited, but I think I managed all right; he seemed to approve. After Bryce rolled out of the van, it was my job to push him up a steep hill along a gravel road to the place where we would get our picture taken. I don't know if you have ever pushed a wheelchair through gravel before, but it's very difficult. Maybe not as bad as trudging through quicksand but still quite the workout!

On top of those challenges, Bryce was the son of the two people running the retreat, so everyone would be paying attention. That meant as I was pushing Bryce's wheelchair up that steep hill, through gravel, his parents, all of the staff, and all of the STMs were watching. All I could think was, *You're going to slip. Bryce is going to fly down the hill and hit a bunch of people. He is going to get hurt, they are going to get hurt, and you are going to be the worst STM to ever walk on the face of the planet!*

Thankfully, those irrational fears did not become realities.

After we got our picture taken together, Bryce wanted to go back down the hill and help greet all the other arriving families.

Being a good STM, I pushed Bryce's wheelchair back down the gravel road, and we sat on the grass yelling and cheering for each family that drove up. I was excited to be there helping Bryce, and I expected God to teach me some pretty cool things.

And he did. Bryce and I ended up having an amazing week filled with incredible memories. Bryce has slight autism, so if I'd told him that it was raining cats and dogs, he would roll his wheelchair to the window and look for cats and dogs falling out of the sky. But Bryce was also very capable of communicating with me and interacting with people at the retreat. He told jokes, he taught me about jazz music, and he called me his slave. (Bryce insisted that STM was really supposed to be MTS, and stood for My Total Slave.)

Confronting My Own Brokenness

But my greatest awakening didn't come from Bryce or his family; it came when I met John.

I couldn't help but stare across the lawn and through the car window at his disfigured appearance. He was the obvious victim of a severe burn and was missing both arms and one leg. I was not overcome with mercy and compassion when I saw John for the first time—I just stared.

Then I began to feel sick—not because of John, but because of the way I responded to him. God was gently but firmly pointing out that my love and acceptance of someone was conditional, based on appearance. I was like the judge of a modeling competition, but instead of using my eyes to judge someone's skill, I was judging someone's worth. As the van pulled away, I was left staring at the brokenness of my heart. I was disgusted at my own lack of love and compassion. What a disfigured, mangled, and evil heart I have!

I found out later that his story was quite amazing. At the time of his accident, he was engaged to be married. Although most of us would be tempted to walk out after such a horrific event, his faithful fiancée stuck with him. They are now married and have three beautiful kids. Her love and commitment to him were stronger than any change in appearance, and seeing the way she loved him reinforced how far I still had to go to become more like Jesus.

A Memorable Moment with Mary

Another unforgettable camper was Mary, whose Down syndrome and vivacious personality played a big role in one of the most interesting moments of the week.

"Sit down and stay there," she said to her mom and two helpers as she pointed to the front row of the auditorium—twenty or so seats away from me.

"Okay, Mary," they said, "we will sit here, but we really want to listen to you play piano."

"You can listen from down here."

As she walked up to the baby grand piano, I could tell that she noticed me and wanted me to notice her. I walked up and asked her if I could play the piano with her. Her entire face lit up into a smile, and she moved over on the piano bench. I sat down, and we began to play.

At first, there was more than a Bible's width between us. But as we started playing, she scooted closer and closer. Soon she was sitting right next to me, and a moment later she laid her head on my shoulder. We kept playing for a couple more minutes until she lifted up her head and kissed my shoulder.

An Unexpected Demand

Not wanting things to go any further, I got up from the piano and told Mary, "Thank you." Most people would have looked back and said, "You're welcome." But she looked back at me and said, "Marry me!"

Caught completely off guard, I replied, "I'm sorry, Mary, but I'm already taken. I'm not available. I'm already married—my wife, Rebecca, is back home with our kids."

"Dump her!" Mary said sternly and emphatically.

"I'm sorry, Mary, but it doesn't work that way."

"Dump her!" she said again—eliciting giggles from her mom and helpers. Finally, her mom got up and came to my aid.

"Come on, Mary," she said. "Daniel can't dump his wife. Let's go."

"I can't marry you, Mary, but we can be best friends," I said to her as she walked off the stage. But she didn't want the infamous "let's be friends" speech; she wanted and expected me to dump my wife and marry her instead.

Social Norms and Family History

"Mary is boy crazy," her mom explained. "I think it has to do with the fact that her dad has never been in the picture, and she is craving that positive male affection in her life. I keep discouraging her from being so friendly with random guys because one day it could be the wrong guy."

"I don't mind," I responded. "That's why we are here this week, so that she can get that positive affection."

Just like most people affected by IDDs, Mary didn't understand appropriate or "normal" social behavior. After knowing me for less than five minutes, she kissed my shoulder and asked me to dump my wife and marry her. But there was another reason she thought it was as simple as me "dumping my wife"—her dad had done the same thing to her and her mom. Mary broke several social norms during our piano duet, yet even after her mom stepped in to explain the situation, she didn't understand.

Down syndrome, autism, and other intellectual and developmental disabilities—not only does each have a spectrum of severity, but each one also brings with it a unique set of struggles and needs.

VALUABLE LESSONS IN ETIQUETTE

One of the greatest benefits from the Joni and Friends Family Retreat was the training we received before families arrived. Rachel did a stellar job of delivering tips and advice that I had never heard before—and I believe it's valuable information for you to know too. A big reason I now feel more confident about spending time with people affected by disabilities is because of the training I received before the retreat started.

Here are some of the highlights Rachel taught us.

What You Say Matters—a Lot

Rachel told us that in her mind, the word *retard* is equivalent to a cussword. She told us that no one should ever use that word and that it breaks her heart anytime someone says it. "Don't do it!" she threatened. "If you do, I will send you home right away!" And watch out for bad terminology. Phrases like "I'm going crazy" are simply inappropriate.

Every day there are cases of someone bullying a fellow classmate who has a disability. This is despicable in every way. Bullying is never okay, but it's especially evil when the recipient is a special-needs student. Making fun of or picking on someone with a disability is like pulling a walker out of an old person's hands or spitting in someone's face—it's never funny and never okay.

Always Get to Know the Person First, Not the Disability

If you talk about the disability first, you are putting a label on that person and devaluing him or her as a person. Don't start a conversation with "What's wrong with her?" or "What's his problem?" or "What does she have?"

Treat the Disabled Person as You Would Any Other Person

Ask the same kinds of questions you would ask anyone else, and strike up a conversation about the same topics. "Hello. How are you? What's your name? What do you like to do for fun? What do you do for a living? Do you have any family?"

Look for Similarities Before Dissimilarities

If they want to talk about their disability, they can bring it up. It's none of our business anyway, and by making it our business, we are proving that they are identified by their disability. Just as we should stay away from racial terms and other labels, we should stay away from treating people affected by disabilities as a label.

Those highlights were all general ideas that can apply in all situations. Rachel then jumped into a series of etiquette topics that related more directly to certain disabilities.

Respect the Role of Working Dogs

"Repeat after me," Rachel told us. "Working dogs are working dogs and not to be petted or played with. It doesn't matter how cute a child's black Labrador retriever is—don't pet it. Don't make eye contact with the dog, don't whistle for the dog to come, and don't pet the dog when you walk by. Let's say it again: working dogs are working dogs and not to be petted or played with.

"Remember that this dog is there to help guide a person with a visual impairment. Regardless of how well trained the dog is, if you call a Labrador, it will behave like a Labrador. It will think that you are supposed to be its new best friend and come running, dragging the poor child with a disability behind. Or worse, leaving the child with a disability alone, panicking because their eyes have run away."

As human beings, we are trained to pet dogs, especially if it is someone else's dog. Rachel made it clear to us that this is not good etiquette when it comes to trained dogs whose role is to help someone with a visual impairment or other disability. Don't pet the dog. Resist the temptation.

Understand Wheelchair Etiquette

The most surprising thing Rachel said about wheelchairs was that they are personal space. She called the chair "an extension of the person." Don't hang on their chairs, touch their chairs, or mess with their chairs without them telling you to. It would be like someone coming up to you and petting your legs—the things you get around on—without your permission. That's both a little weird and a little freaky.

Bryce was often used as the class example. Rachel would pull him up in front of the class and show us all of the things not to do. At the same time, she also used Bryce to show us the way to interact with people in wheelchairs.

"Start by getting down on their level," she said. "Squat down so that you can talk to them in the eyes, and show them how important they are to you. Also, try to remember to shake their hand, and if appropriate, give them a hug or some other form of positive human contact. Surprisingly, people in wheelchairs hardly ever get any form of human contact—people just don't think about it. You can make a huge impact on someone in a chair just by shaking hands with them and, if you know them well enough, by giving them a hug."

Understand More About Autism and Other IDDs

Finally, Rachel talked to us about intellectual and developmental disabilities—specifically autism.

"Now, let me tell you a little bit about autism because a lot of the kids you will be interacting with this week have different degrees of autism. First, autism affects communication, social interaction, and sensory experience. Out of respect for them, don't finish their sentences; be patient and let them say a complete thought. By interrupting them, you are not honoring them. Even if the conversation is incredibly slow and broken, don't cut in— you're here to listen to them.

"Secondly, people affected by autism have 'stims,' which are repetitious movements or things that they will do so that they can feel something or keep themselves from being bored. You will notice that my son spins in his chair and listens to jazz music. This is his stim.

"Thirdly, don't act like you understand what they are saying if you don't understand what they are saying. Don't guess. Don't just say, 'Yes' or 'Uh-huh.' If you need help understanding them, find a leader or their caretaker."

I hope these etiquette highlights can be as helpful to you as they've been to me. I have seen numerous people affected by disabilities in the grocery store or at church and had no idea what to do or say. But by ignoring someone affected by a disability, we are ignoring someone whom God knit together in her mother's womb (see Psalm 139:13)—someone who is God's workmanship (see Ephesians 2:10).

TIME FOR ACTION

Going ten days without legs will be a life-changing experience for you. I believe that far too many people don't know what to do or how to help those affected by disabilities. The real problem is not that we lack a cure; the problem is that we are not taught how to love and take care of people who may have special needs. And we rarely look for opportunities to serve and interact with those individuals.

Find the Right Opportunity

Obviously, I'm a big fan of Joni and Friends. It's an organization that is committed to accelerating Christian outreach to the disability community. Part of that commitment is to bridge the gap by creating awareness and engaging people in genuine, heartfelt ministry with those affected by disabilities. But maybe your church has a ministry with a similar commitment. Perhaps a local parachurch organization is dedicated to this cause. Simply connect with folks who have a heart for faithfully and respectfully serving this amazing group of people.

Share the Message

Inform people about your challenge—and why you're doing it. Spread the word on social media, send out e-mails or letters, and let your friends, family, coworkers, and acquaintances know how they can get involved in the cause. The more people who serve, the greater impact you can have on individuals and families living with disabilities.

By the way, here's an important health note if you're going to replicate my Ten Days Without Legs experiment: I was advised by two nurses—my mother-in-law and a friend of mine—that spending ten straight days in a wheelchair without a break can be risky to someone with two good legs. They recommended standing up for a five-minute break once every two hours. And considering how much I trust their expert opinions, I pass along this same advice to you!

A Change of Heart

Before I end this chapter, I want to go back and finish telling you about John.

On the last day of the retreat, things were different. I can't say that somehow John's scars became beautiful or that something switched in my brain so that I found his appearance pleasing. But something had changed in my heart.

During the retreat, I made it a priority to talk to him as much as possible. Shocked at my reaction to him on my first day of the retreat, I knew that I needed to get to know John as a person. I was not serving his family that week, which meant I didn't get much time to spend with him, but during free time or when I had the chance, I always said "Hi" and asked how he was doing.

As I walked by his wheelchair on the last day of the family retreat, I noticed that his son, who was about the same age as my son, was asleep on John's shoulder. I mean this kid was out—completely asleep and completely at peace. His son didn't care what his dad looked like or that his dad had only half an arm to hold him with; John was his daddy, and his daddy was the most comfortable and secure place to be in the entire world.

"There's nothing like having your boy sleep on you, is there, John?" I half said and half asked.

"Nope! Nothing like it," he replied.

At that moment I realized that John and I are the same in many ways. We both love it when our kids fall asleep in our arms, and we both love our families deeply and passionately. That was the moment when I finally got past what John looked like and began caring about a guy who was a lover to his wife and a hero to his boys. John could have felt sorry for himself, but instead he has mastered the harmonica and knows the Bible inside and out. Instead of questioning the sovereignty of God, John wants to use his disability to bring people closer to God.

Before the retreat, I would not have gotten past the way John looked to understand his personality or talents. Instead, I would have stared—ignoring someone whom God cares about. Out of concern for saying the wrong thing, I would have said nothing. And I also would have missed out on interacting with the workmanship of God.

As you go ten days without legs, may God open your eyes and challenge your heart just as he did mine.

7

Waste Not, Want Not

Ten Days Without Waste
to Address the Environment

➤ ➤ ➤ The earth is the LORD's, and everything in it, the
world, and all who live in it.

PSALM 24:1

*y name is Daniel Day, and I'm going ten days without waste to
raise money to train farmers in the developing world. For the
next ten days I will not be throwing anything away in a trash can. I
will use only recyclable or compostable materials. Ten days. No waste.
Starts now.*

Day 3…Ever had one of those days when the cold seems
to penetrate your skin all the way down to your bones?
You try to warm up your hands, but just moments after
you warm them up they're cold again. You sit down by a
heater, but the heat is too localized and can't seem to reach
you. The weather doesn't even have to be that cold outside,
yet cold just seems to hit you the wrong way.

For me, this morning was one of those mornings. I

walked into the office, pulled off my coat, and immediately the cold started seeping into my arms. Normally this isn't a problem because I can quickly make a cup of coffee and let it heat me up from the inside out. But today I was faced with a dilemma: How do I make a cup of coffee without waste?

My cup is not the problem. It's porcelain. I can use that cup over and over again without causing any waste. My problem is the filter. I know that for certain coffee makers you can buy reusable filters, but I don't have a coffee maker—I'm a pour-over guy.

I don't know that I've ever stopped to think about the fact that I throw away a paper coffee filter every day. I bet all of us would be surprised by how many little things we throw away. I'm not saying that it's a bad thing to throw away coffee filters, but what if there's a good alternative? I've never actually looked into it before, so maybe today is a good day to do just that.

The Bible, the Christian, and the Environment

Much of the American church struggles with our role on this planet. We know we're called to be good, effective stewards over the earth, but we instead focus our energy on the "dominion" side of things. In the name of consumerism and excess, we've adopted the mentality that "wealthiness" is next to godliness, regardless of who or what we destroy along the way.

I'll confess that on plenty of occasions the only "green" things I cared about were Kermit the Frog, Oscar the Grouch, and the greenbacks padding (or absent from) my wallet. Instead of caring about the environment, I treated environmentalism as inconvenient and lacking science and a cause supported by a bunch of quacks who have issues. With exploration of Scripture and a broader perspective of the world, however, my attitudes have changed.

A Biblical Foundation

Our stewardship of the earth is rooted in Genesis 1:26–28:

> Then God said, "Let us make man in our image, in our likeness, and let them rule over the fish of the sea and the birds of the air, over the livestock, over all the earth, and over all the creatures that move along the ground."
>
> So God created man in his own image,
> > in the image of God he created him;
> > male and female he created them.
>
> God blessed them and said to them, "Be fruitful and increase in number; fill the earth and subdue it. Rule over the fish of the sea and the birds of the air and over every living creature that moves on the ground."

When many people read the words "rule" and "subdue," they picture a buffet line at their favorite restaurant. (All-you-can-eat pizza? Count me in!) For some reason, they think subduing the earth means getting the most for our money by consuming with no thought to the pending consequences of wasteful living. After all, how many people go to a buffet and eat only one plate of food?

But when God told humanity to "rule" over the earth, he used the Hebrew word *radah*, which simply means "to have dominion over."[22] God was not telling us to consume at will; God was telling us that we are responsible for the earth, like a manager or steward.

And as stewards, we ought to care for the earth as if we were managing a business—to help it flourish and thrive for the glory of the owner. That's what we as Christians should want for the earth: to take such good care of it that it brings glory and honor to the one who created it.

Caring for God's Masterpiece

Read the first chapter of Genesis, and you'll see the effort and creativity that God poured into creating the world. The account of creation should cause us to feel a burning desire and passionate commitment to care for this amazing gift. It's as if the sixth day of creation was the first Christmas morning and God gave humanity the two greatest gifts ever: life and an amazing place to live. It makes sense that we should take care of those gifts.

Unfortunately, too many Christians in Western culture read the opening pages of Scripture and believe God demands that we consume everything like a swarm of locusts in a wheat field, with little regard for how today's choices will affect our children, our grandchildren, and generations to come—or how our choices *already are affecting* people who speak languages we don't understand, in nations we'll never visit. As long as we're fat and happy and prosperous, we remain content to lounge in our apathy and consumerism.

But what if the way we treat our planet really *does* matter? What if when God said it was "very good," he meant the fruit trees, lakes, and mountains just as much as the human beings he put in charge of it all? What if he really did look at all of creation and was blown away by his own masterpiece? It would explain why he had to take a day off after he was done.

Consider this: I live in Colorado near Pikes Peak. If you've ever driven to Colorado from the east, you've experienced the amazing sight of the Rocky Mountains rising up out of the horizon. (You also probably have toyed with the idea of moving to this stunningly beautiful state!) Every day as I drive into work, I'm blown away by the grandness and beauty of the Rockies—except for one blemish that I try to ignore. To the right of Pikes Peak sits an old quarry mine that rips an ugly hole in the landscape. Looking at the tear in the mountain makes me feel like something is missing—a piece of beauty is gone. I'm not here to debate whether surface mines are morally wrong, but when you see a mine break up a beautiful mountain range, it sure doesn't feel right.

Please understand: I am not an expert on earth maintenance any more than I am an expert on car maintenance. I can change my oil and replace wiper blades, but after that I get lost. When it comes to concepts like climate change, global warming, and other politically charged topics, I don't always know who's telling the truth. But I do believe God wants us to lead lives that are defined not by waste or excess or selfishness or consumerism but by stewardship and responsibility and generosity and modest living.

And I believe that by constantly ignoring or downplaying the cause of stewardship, the American church has hurt its reputation and standing with people who care about the environment. Our isolation and apathy limit our influence in reaching the culture with the message of Jesus.

OUR LEGACY: A CULTURE OF WASTE

I created a lot of confusion when I declared that I would be going ten days without waste. For some reason, many people thought that I was going to avoid using a toilet for ten days. Um, no. Clearly I had been misunderstood! Ten Days Without Waste was about removing trash and excess and garbage from my life—and becoming aware of all the wasteful packaging I normally buy and how much stuff I throw away.

I remember going into a fast-food restaurant for lunch during one of those ten days. As I looked over the menu and prepared to order, I asked myself, "How is this meal going to be presented to me?" Realizing that ordering a meal meant receiving a noncompostable cup and a load of trash, I had to walk out without buying anything (and without taking home any special toys for my kids—sad day, indeed).

When you start paying attention, you'll be amazed when you realize how much you waste in an average day. Tissues. Leftovers. Wrappers. Napkins. Packaging. Empty toothpaste tubes. And even those of us who make a concerted effort to recycle still produce plenty of garbage. (This next week, see which fills up faster: your recycling bin or your trash can.)

Is it possible to make an entire grocery visit and purchase only items that create no waste? Can you run a household using no products that end up in the garbage? Can you throw a birthday party without filling up bags of trash?

Well, that last one turned out to be easier than I thought.

Wasteless Celebration

The funniest day of the experiment came on my twenty-fifth birthday, which landed during my ten days without waste. My wife planned a themed party and was careful to buy only things that were compostable, reusable, or recyclable. It was great!

Peanut shells, chocolate cake, and Nerf darts covered the carpet, while empty bottles of root beer, plastic guns, and recycled cardboard saloon doors decorated our kitchen for my cowboy-and-Indian party at our house. What can I say? Ever since my last party with that theme (back in elementary school), I'd wanted to have another one.

I had an amazing time watching my grown-up friends shoot each other with Nerf guns, put up their hair in pigtails, and drink bottles of root beer. It was hilarious to watch them release their inner children, and I had a fantastic night.

How did we have that much fun without creating a lot of waste? We composted the peanut shells and paper plates. Rebecca bought glass-bottled root beer so we could recycle the bottles (and for the effect, of course—nothing says "frontier" like brown root-beer bottles and candy cigars). And all of the food was reheatable or compostable. After an entire birthday party with seventeen adults and nine and a half children (the half is for our friend who was pregnant—she deserves some credit), only a third of our thirteen-gallon trash can was full. In fact, the only things we needed to throw away were a tablecloth that evidently couldn't be recycled and some plastic packaging for the fruit. (Come on, fruit companies—become more sustainable!)

Here's the deal: Yes, we still ended up with a few items of trash here and there, but amazingly, we did not fill one trash bag throughout the entire ten days of my challenge. It took effort. It required intentional shopping. It demanded thoughtful trips through the grocery store, cooperation in the kitchen, and an all-in attitude from my family and friends.

Was it easy? Nope. Was it possible? Absolutely.

Now that's stewardship.

HELPING FARMERS CARE FOR THE EARTH

But being a steward of the world is not just an American problem—it's a global problem. If you visit other nations, you will see poor stewardship of the earth, including in the developing world. I remember driving on the highway in Honduras, disgusted by the amount of trash littering the sides of the streets.

We hear about the Amazon and how the rainforest is being deforested. We hear about how Japanese whalers continue to hunt. We see documentaries about the piles of trash in India's slums. And Mexico City has long held the reputation for the smoggiest city in the world. Environmentalism is definitely a global issue. But how can we help?

Perhaps we can't change the policies in other nations, but we can do something specific and tangible: help address the needs facing many farmers in parts of the developing world. Far too many farmers in these nations are not well trained in agriculture. They don't understand the importance of letting the earth rest or the consequences of stripping the ground of its resources. In many countries, crop rotations and good irrigation simply don't exist, and as a result, either crops don't grow or the yield is small—too small to provide for a family and sell in the market.

For a farmer in the developing world who depends on crops to provide food and money for his family, understanding good farming techniques is vital to escaping poverty—the issues are closely interwoven. Yet as we survey the landscape of agriculture in the developing world, we see many farmers getting further and further behind.

Not only are too many farmers uneducated and missing out on the ability to maximize their farms, but they are also left with largely unusable land. When I was in Honduras, one of the poor farmers I met owned a hillside—and that was it. Hillside farming is incredibly difficult (how's that for an understatement?), and he needed someone to teach him how to do it. But no one was there to help, and instead of flourishing, this guy's efforts at farming can't feed his family or help them escape extreme poverty.

That's why my ten days without waste was about more than just removing waste from my life and waking people up to their call to stewardship. It was also about introducing people to organizations that fight poverty through environmentalism. Although I wanted to use this experiment as a fund-raiser for those organizations, I found that most of my blog followers simply needed to know that they existed. Not much money was raised during those ten days, but I was able to introduce a lot of people to groups like Plant With Purpose—an organization that not only helps plant trees but also educates farmers in the developing world. So when I went to find an organization to sponsor, this one fit the criteria beautifully.

TIME FOR ACTION

I believe Ten Days Without Waste is a worthwhile challenge, even if you already do a lot of the things I've discussed in this chapter. We all need a little help becoming better stewards of the earth, and we all need to experiment with the joy of reducing, recycling, and reusing. (Yes, I use the word *joy* to describe it!)

I encourage you to support an organization like Plant With Purpose that is investing resources in training and equipping farmers in developing nations. Get other people involved and aware, and look for ways to turn your waste-reducing experiment into a lifelong habit.

I do want to pass along some additional ideas on how you can remove a little bit of waste in your life. These suggestions come from my wife, who did Ten Days Without Waste with me because, obviously, we share the same house and groceries.

There is nothing my husband hates more than coming home to an overflowing trash can. Over the past four-plus years of our marriage, many comical quarrels have taken place around trash. When I was growing up, my dad and brother took out the trash—case (or lid) closed. My mother, my three sisters, and I *never* had to even think about trash. Unfortunately, as with many other things in marriage, Daniel and I did not have the same expectations.

It's not that he won't take out the trash. It's that I'm the one home all day filling it up to overflowing. By the time Daniel gets home to see the K2 of trash piles, he would rather turn a blind eye to the behemoth, which makes me want to strangle him.

So I was very excited about this challenge. It helped better our marriage, raised money for others, and has taken us one step closer toward restoring our planet to its God given beauty.

Here are a few specific things I have been doing at home to cut down on the amount of waste:

- *Changing our habits with diapers.* Being a mother of two boys makes things interesting. Being a mother of two boys still in diapers makes things disgusting. I have found poop in unimaginable places: behind their ears, below their toes, in my bed, and even on my walls. So when we made the switch to cloth diapers a few months ago, we were both a bit skeptical—but being on a tight budget and hearing great reports about it, we decided to give it a go. Seven months later we have helped cut down on the billions of disposable diapers dumped into landfills each year and have enjoyed doing it!

- *Buying mostly fruits and vegetables.* We now do our best to buy food without packaging.
- *Avoiding those plastic produce and checkout bags and bringing my own reusable bags.*
- *Composting food scraps, paper products, coffee filters, and other appropriate items.*
- *Repurposing waste.* We turn old shirts into rags or sew them into blankets, and we use boxes for storage and glass containers for cups.
- *Adopting new bathroom patterns.* We flush the toilet less often (with discretion!), fill the sink instead of continuously running the water, and bathe the babies in the sink instead of the tub. We also try to take shorter showers.

It is amazing how simple it is to reduce waste and how rewarding it is at the same time. Give it a try!

OPEN THE DOOR FOR THE GOSPEL

Reducing waste and being a steward of the earth and our resources simply means being a good manager of the earth we have been given. I believe God cares about the earth and the way we govern, and I think we have the opportunity to honor God with the way we "rule."

James Davison Hunter, in his book *To Change the World*, has a powerful quote. He says:

> Rather than being defined by its cultural achievements, its intellectual and artistic vitality, its service to the needs of others, Christianity is defined to the outside world by its rhetoric of resentment and the ambitions of a will in opposition to others.[23]

Although Hunter's statement is somewhat of a sweeping generalization and should therefore be scrutinized, I think there is some truth to what he is saying, especially in regard to environmentalism. For decades, Christians have shown the world that we don't care about the earth or the environment by proclaiming, "The earth is not our home." With an escapist mentality, we have neglected our responsibility as stewards and have painted a negative image of our faith to an entire group of scientists, politicians, and environmental activists.

I think that by becoming environmentalists, we Christians are not just living out our God-ordained responsibility as the earth's managers, but we will also be opening up a very large door for the gospel. Love with a hidden agenda is not love, of course. We shouldn't start caring about the environment so that we can proselytize and turn people off that way. But we should all take seriously our mandate to "rule over the fish of the sea and the birds of the air and over every living creature that moves on the ground"

(Genesis 1:28). Here's what I know: farmers in the developing world need better education to grow better and healthier crops. They need fruit trees to grow, but many of them can't afford to buy those trees. We can help organizations that are meeting this need, providing the necessary training and resources, and making a tangible difference.

And just as importantly, I know that I use too much trash and waste too much food. I know that I can recycle more and reuse more. I know that I can be more careful with the amount of water I leave running and can turn off lights in unoccupied rooms. Let's do our part to steward the earth wherever we can—and our homes are great places to start.

My wife and I are still very conscious of what we throw away, even two years after the experiment. We still watch how much water we use. And we stopped using paper towels altogether. We have several cloth rags that we use and wash instead.

8

Freedom Through Silence

Ten Days Without Speech to Address Modern-Day Slavery

➤ ➤ ➤ The Spirit of the Lord is on me, because he has anointed me to preach good news to the poor. He has sent me to proclaim freedom for the prisoners and recovery of sight for the blind, to release the oppressed, to proclaim the year of the Lord's favor.

LUKE 4:18–19

My name is Daniel Day, and I'm going ten days without using my voice to be a voice for victims of human trafficking and slavery around the world. For the next ten days I will not be talking. I will carry a whiteboard around to communicate with people. Ten days. No speech. Starts now.

Day 5…"Daddy, TALK TO ME," yells Noah, my two-year-old son. He wants me to read him a story instead of only showing him the pictures. Quickly, my wife steps in to try to explain why daddy's not talking.

"Daddy can't talk," she says. "Remember how we keep

talking about kids who don't get to play because bad men are forcing them to make bricks or pick rice instead?"

Noah nods and says, "We poke bad men in the eyes!"

"You're right, we poke bad men in the eyes," she says, and we both laugh. "Daddy is trying to raise money to send people to save those boys and girls. You see, those boys and girls can't look at the bad men and say, 'Stop hurting us and making us work,' because the bad men don't listen to them. Daddy's not using his voice to be a voice for those boys and girls."

"Well, I'm not using my voice for ten days," Noah replies. Rebecca and I look at each other, and we know each other's thought: In some ways, Noah not being able to ask, "Why, why, why, why, why, why, why, why" wouldn't be the worst thing in the world. At the same time, it's amazing to see his childlike sensitivity to others who are hurting.

Rebecca looks at Noah and says, "Okay, you can do that if you want, but now it's time to go to bed!"

Thinking that he can get out of a nap, Noah responds, "I'm going ten days without my bed."

Rebecca's mommy-wit kicks in: "Okay, you can sleep on the floor if you want." The disappointment is evident on Noah's face as he realizes that his strategy has failed. He slouches his shoulders, turns around, and heads for the stairs.

After an hour or so of excuses, Noah finally goes to sleep, and I'm left wondering why I'm doing this. But then

I think about my boys sleeping comfortably in their beds—free from the modern-day slavery that ensnares millions of children in our world, children who are forced to work in brickyards or rice fields instead of being allowed to take naps.

If my small sacrifice of silence can help raise money that could pull those kids out of slavery, it's all worth it!

WITHOUT A VOICE, WE HAVE NO POWER

Overall, Ten Days Without Speech was the hardest challenge that I did. Most people are surprised by that, but think about it: our voices give us power—power to influence people to our points of view, power to stand up for ourselves during life's most crucial moments, and power to get people's attention during the most mundane. (The drive-through window is completely out of the question—but even eating inside a restaurant is tough when you aren't speaking!)

But what happens when we lose that power? What happens when we lose our ability to make our ideas known, defend ourselves, ask for help? What happens to even simple communication? What if our voices are taken away, like they have been for the twenty-seven million slaves around the world?

The first time I heard someone talk about modern-day slavery, I didn't believe it was true. In my mind, slavery and human trafficking existed only in history books or painful memories; the modern world had moved away from such archaic inhumanity. I was so blinded to the existence of these travesties that when I began working on the Ten Days Without project, those issues weren't even on my radar. Sure, I had heard of organizations like International Justice Mission, but only in passing.

I know what you're wondering: *Did he live under a rock?* Maybe! It's embarrassing to admit that a guy who works for a Christian ministry, grew up in a Christian home, attended a Christian school, and served at a Christian church didn't know that slavery still exists.

But I know now, and that knowledge changes the way I view everything.

A Coffeehouse "Conversation"

"Sorry about the wait," the young barista said, apologizing for the extra three minutes I'd been waiting in line. "What can I get for you today?"

I felt like I needed to offer my own apology about the wait as I pulled out my mini whiteboard and began writing my order. (Yes, I should've written it ahead of time, but I was suffering from severe caffeine deprivation.) Normally when I walk into a coffee shop, it takes only a moment to order coffee, but not when I'm going ten days without speaking—*everything* takes longer!

As I finished writing my order, she read the statement written on top of the whiteboard: "I'm not using my voice today to be a voice for two million children around the world stuck in the commercial sex trade."

"Oh, that's cool," she said. "How many days are you doing this?" I didn't have the heart to point out the big black letters on the bottom of the board that read, "10DaysWithout.com." Instead, I graciously erased my order and wrote, "Ten days, but tomorrow is my last day."

"Wow! That's amazing," she said. "I don't think I could do it for one day. I'd just end up talking to myself the whole time."

No joke! I went from being able to talk to everybody to not being able to talk to anybody, including my reflection in the mirror. I could sympathize with the young woman behind the counter, even if I didn't take the opportunity to admit it.

I erased my purple markings and wrote, "It's very hard!"

"I bet!" she responded. "Good luck!"

Speaking Up for the Voiceless

Luck. What a fascinating word. Some people might say I was lucky to have been born in a nation where my freedoms are protected and my voice is heard. I consider it a blessing, but it's also a responsibility. Those of us with voices have an obligation, a duty, a charge to stand up for those who don't. And that's what Ten Days Without Speech is really all about.

It's a responsibility rooted in biblical truth. God tells us, "Seek justice, encourage the oppressed. Defend the cause of the fatherless, plead the case of the widow" (Isaiah 1:17). And later in the Old Testament, we read, "And what does the LORD require of you? To act justly and to love mercy and to walk humbly with your God" (Micah 6:8).

God cares about justice and helping the oppressed. God wants us to stand up and use our voices to set the captive free. Though times have changed since the Bible was written, there is still injustice in this world. God wants us to promote love and pursue justice.

LEARNING MORE ABOUT MODERN-DAY SLAVERY

It's increasingly easy to study the statistics about the problems of human trafficking and modern-day slavery. But the stats weren't primarily responsible for changing my perspective on these issues or making the problem real to me. It was hearing about the problem from some of the people who fight against it every day at International Justice Mission (IJM.org), a nonprofit organization that works on behalf of victims of slavery, sexual exploitation, and other forms of violent oppression.

I arranged a visit to IJM's Washington, DC, offices in September 2012 to do research on slavery and human trafficking around the globe. While there, I had the privilege of talking with several key staff members responsible for different areas of IJM's response to these difficult issues.

What does modern-day slavery look like? That was my foundational question for my first conversation of the day. After all, if almost every country in the world has a law against it, it shouldn't exist, right?

Sadly, it does still exist, though its forms and methods have changed in recent times. Saju Mathew, the director of operations for South Asia, explained that centuries ago the slave trade was a business—a legal transaction of human beings as property that was condoned and endorsed by governments and businessmen.

"It was a visible way of functioning, it was normalized, and they didn't see anything wrong with it," he said, a tragic but honest assessment. "The challenge back then for abolitionists was enacting laws to make it illegal and then doing whatever it took after the laws were in place to eradicate the practice of slavery."

As he began to explain what slavery looks like today, I slid forward in my seat. If you've ever sat in conversation with an expert before, you know the feeling of being drawn into that person's experience and knowledge.

Ancient Crime, New Strategies

Laws ban slavery around the world, yet the practice continues. How is this possible?

"The slave owners just disguise it in new ways," Saju said. "In South Asia, where I lead teams that free slaves, slavery never really went away. It just morphed into a different form: debt bondage. When slavery was declared illegal, slave owners no longer had the freedom to do it publically and needed to find a way to make the process look legitimate.

"They began by offering someone a little bit of money up front in exchange for a promise to work for them, which they call an advance. A business owner explains it to the potential slave like this: 'You come work for me at my place. I will pay you for the work, you use that money to live and pay off the debt, and when you're done you can leave.'"

That sounds like a pretty good deal—except that it's a scheme. The worker is required to live on site, and the employer often creates a work schedule that gives little freedom and requires long hours. For example, people working in a rice field will find themselves drying the rice during the day and boiling it at night. They might get a brief break in the morning, but most of the time that they're awake, they're working. How's that for a raw deal?

Most of the laborers aren't educated, which compounds the problems. They can't read, and they don't understand basic math, leaving them highly vulnerable to exploitation.

"I've asked a man who is clearly forty or more how old he is, and he will say four or twelve," Saju said. "He has no concept of numbers. So when you talk about a business owner giving them advance money and telling them, 'You received this much, this much you owe, this is how much I'm giving you, and I'm subtracting this much from your advance,' it's very easy to confuse them."

Still another complicating factor is the caste system in many of these countries that creates rigid social boundaries based on race, birth, and wealth. Workers don't feel empowered to question the employers' demands, even when they're unreasonable.

Basic Freedoms Begin to Disappear

"Just like most schemes, initially the deal looks fine, and then slowly—like a frog in a pot of water—the rules change," Saju said. "It's never traumatic right away, only over time."

In other words, when the worker asks for permission to go back to his community because a relative is sick or to take care of a personal issue, the employer says no. At that moment, everything changes.

"All of a sudden the laborer needs permission to do anything and everything, and the owner is actually controlling the things in the laborer's life that they never handed over to them in the first place," Saju told me. "Basic freedoms are taken away so that now you can't go to the market without getting permission. If you want to go to the market, you can only go on this day. And if you want to buy something, you have to be supervised by someone else. Or you can leave a child back with the owner. Or you can only go to this one particular stall to buy provisions, which just so happens to also be owned by the business owner. So they find themselves gradually trapped inside a system that is not really built by walls or chains but just by these rules and confinement that they have to operate under—rules and confinement that they never agreed to work under in the first place."

At this point in the situation, most of us would make a run for it. I know that I would! Or we'd find a new employer. Or we'd do *something* to escape such a horrible arrangement. Saju said that some workers manage to return to their villages but are often tracked down. And some of the workers have families and can't run in the first place without fear of what will happen to their relatives.

Modern-day slavery may look and function differently than the system in past centuries, but it's still slavery.

"Whenever a person's basic freedoms are taken away, that's slavery," Saju said. "Instead of a public trading block, we have these laborers with no power, no voice, no one to advocate for them, no understanding of the law, trapped there, and they have to live there, and their families are there, and their debts are constantly increasing—that's modern-day slavery."

CONFRONTING HUMAN TRAFFICKING

Later that day at the IJM offices, I spoke with Christa Hayden, who specializes in aftercare for underage girls rescued from brothels. She was moving back to Cambodia to work with girls ages five to twenty-two, who have been trafficked into sexual slavery. As our conversation began, she told me the story of a little girl whose actions reminded Christa of the boy in the Bible who offered his loaves and fish to Jesus, who then used that small gift to miraculously feed thousands of people.

"She didn't have much to give—but everything she did have to give, she gave," Christa said. "We did an operation in Cambodia with the police to rescue girls who had been trafficked to a brothel, and a girl who was rescued began sharing with social workers about an American man who was also a professor at a local university. She was first sold to him, and when he was finished with her, she was then sold to the brothel. She still had friends who were enslaved at that man's house, and she wanted to see those girls rescued."

This young girl boldly led the team to the man's house, where he was keeping four girls: an eighteen-year-old, an eleven-year-old, and two sisters, ages nine and ten. IJM worked with the US embassy and the Cambodian anti-human-trafficking police to successfully rescue those girls and arrest the trafficker.

At the same time, the team was investigating reports of another pedophile in the community, and when law enforcement raided the man's home, they found two girls, an eleven-year-old and a twelve-year-old, who had been forced into prostitution at the man's beachside club.

Celebrating in the Sea

"Yet these girls had never visited the actual beach or seen the water," Christa said.

"Later, when we were at the police station, the Cambodian social workers and I were assessing the girls' emergency needs, asking them, 'What do you need? Water? Medicine? Food?' and they said, 'The sea! We want to see the sea!' So we did our initial interviews, and then the next morning we got up and had breakfast at the beach so they could see the waves.

"It was funny because they didn't know what to do with the waves and ended up falling over in the water in their pajamas that we gave them. But the most touching part was when they stood up on a rock, with their arms around each other, and stared at the ocean in silence for about twenty minutes until we called them to go. I can only imagine what they were contemplating."

During the drive back to the aftercare home, Christa and her team discovered that these girls knew the other girls who had been rescued just a few weeks earlier. What was the connection? "The American's house," the girls said.

"Finally, we were able to put it all together," Christa said. "The Vietnamese trafficker had found these girls and negotiated their sale from a similar community to the American professor. He would break them and teach them how to have sex. When he was finished with them, he sent them down to the second pedophile at the beach strip club where they were forced to perform publicly.

"But what made this story amazing was not the intricate trafficking ring that we had cracked; it was the fact that during the course of the investigation and operations with the police, these girls wanted to stand up for each other, find out where the other girls—their friends—were, and get them rescued."

And it all began with that one girl who took the risk of showing investigators where the American professor lived.

The story gets better: the girls testified against the perpetrator, and they're now all doing well in their high school classes and experiencing a better life.

Using Their Voices as Best They Can

But I just couldn't shake a vital question. "So would you say that it is accurate to say that these girls don't have a voice?" I asked Christa. "Because it almost sounds like they did have a voice and that they used it for each other."

She thought for a moment and then responded.

"Abused and trafficked girls don't have a voice in regards to large power structures and moving people to take action on their behalf," she said. "They don't have the ability or freedom to escape their bondage, go before their local governments, and get someone to protect them or incarcerate the abusers. So when we talk about this larger voice, you're right—everything about the girls' circumstances tells them they are nothing and the world is against them, and they don't have the ability to stick up for themselves.

"But I don't think these girls would call themselves powerless.

I think about stories that we've read of slaves in the old days where they fought in small ways to keep their family members, or said to themselves, 'I'm going to sing my song of praise or my song of defiance when you can't hear me.'

"We saw that in the case of those girls in Cambodia. The power—the voices—these girls did have, they put into use protecting each other, looking out for each other. The eighteen-year-old girl that we rescued told us that she could have escaped several times but couldn't bear to leave those younger girls. She explained that even though staying meant that she continued to face abuse, she felt she could maybe take some of the focus off of them."

Rekindling the Fire

I was beginning to see how even in the darkest circumstances, people could still use their voices for good. I asked Christa to clarify exactly what she meant in regard to the girls not having a voice.

"I don't want to diminish the power of violence in their lives and the power of rape to diminish who they think they are as a person," Christa said. "These girls are definitely crushed and broken. They recognize that the world is not on their side and that it's never been. Oftentimes their families either haven't been or can't be there for them, community hasn't been or can't, police haven't been or can't, social services hasn't been or can't. Nothing and no one has come on to their side before, and they understand that they are not 'power players.' So in that sense, in the bigger picture, I want to be very clear in saying that they don't have a voice, that they don't have the power to stop the violence perpetrated against them.

"But with that said, there's a small voice and fire in the majority of girls that may be very low lit, but I think that it's there. Aftercare can help weed away all of the lies, pain, years of violence,
nightmares, and shame—to get them to the place where that
small voice, that small fire that exists deep, deep down and has
been covered over and smothered for so long, can finally come
back to life once again."

Christa's passion and love for those girls was mesmerizing. I
had always wanted to be part of a fight, to stand up for those without voices and make a difference in the world. But as I sat there
listening to Christa's story, I was convicted that I have neglected
the freedom and power I've been given. When have I ever used my
voice for others in such dire situations?

RESPONDING TO ABUSIVE POLICE POWER
AND LAND GRABBING

I still had one more meeting left that day, but I didn't need any
more information. I had a good mental picture of what modern-
day slavery looked like, the weight of human trafficking had been
downloaded into my heart, and I didn't know if I could handle
the weight of any more evil and injustice.

When I walked into Philip Langford's office, my eyes immediately darted to the gigantic map of Africa behind him—and I
quickly realized how much geography I had forgotten since high
school.

He told me about abusive police power in Kenya, including
cases where officers had surrounded individual men and forced

them to confess to crimes they hadn't committed—and sometimes this had happened with the men's young children watching. Instead of being the protector and source of security, the police frequently become the source of violence.

"When IJM hears about these kinds of stories, what do you do about it?" I asked. "Do you confront the cops?"

"We have confronted the commanders with their lack of evidence and the maliciousness of their officers," Philip said, "but they often respond, 'Well, let's just let this play out—this is a chance for you, IJM lawyer, to shine in the courtroom.' That level of callousness is mind blowing."

"So what do you do next?" I asked.

"At that point we begin our own investigation and begin building the case for the prisoner's innocence. We represent the prisoner in court and oftentimes get the acquittal. But honestly, getting an acquittal is not enough to change the system. The reason I am so passionate about IJM and want to dedicate my life to this organization is because we are going after the system—not just dirty cops and politicians."

Pursuing Justice and Change

Far too often, Philip told me, police aren't held accountable. They might face a minor penalty if convicted, but that's it. Meanwhile, IJM's clients—the true victims in these situations—are afraid of retribution.

"Doesn't that make you want to go down there and clean up the streets with a gun?" I asked.

"It's funny you say that," he replied, "because a lot of people have a misconception about IJM and think that we go into all of these countries like a bunch of cowboys—slinging lead into corrupt bad guys. But that is *not* our approach at all. We are lawyers, investigators, and social workers, not Walker, Texas Ranger. Instead, we work within the system itself, with the goal of slowly helping the system mature and evolve into an actual justice system with due process."

Legal Fights over Land

Philip went on to tell me about land grabbing—a tragic situation for widows in developing nations in Africa. He said somewhere between 30 percent and 55 percent of orphans and widows are either the victims or intended victims of this cruel practice.

Here's how it works. In a country like Uganda, a woman's identity and security traditionally come through her immediate family and then through her husband. But if her husband dies, she's left with no real identity.

"When he dies, she is essentially dependent on either going to her family or going to the husband's family," Philip said. "But her family says, 'We've already sold you off,' and the husband's family says, 'You're dead to us.' Either way, she is very, very vulnerable."

Officially, a widow has legal rights in many of these nations. But in practice, the in-laws and extended family often act quickly—they move in, kick out the widow and her kids, and take the property.

"There is not a safety blanket or security net for her, and there're no social services available. Before the husband died, they were barely getting by, maybe doing some subsistence agriculture—

just getting enough from their land to take and sell to the market. Maybe they were renting out a portion of the land to someone else. But either way, the land is the sole source of survival—that's it. So if she is kicked off of the land, she has no way to provide for herself or her children."

And if she looks for help from the government or the police or other officials, they'll often tell her it's a family dispute and won't get involved.

"The police are not going to respond even though what has been done to her is a crime," Philip said. "And when we say crime, we mean that it is not just a private offense—it's an offense against the state. In other words, it's so grievous that the state has an interest in regulating it. But what the magistrate or police officers uniformly say is that it is a family matter and the widow needs to go take care of it with her family."

And even if officials do get involved, the cases often end up in mediation, and the offender may still wind up keeping some of the land. That's when IJM gets involved and works on behalf of the widow and her children.

"We have actually resolved a lot of those cases in mediation, but we are convinced that it will not end until there is a higher price to be paid by the perpetrators," Philip told me. "Because if the worst thing that can happen to you is that you end up with some of the land, it actually works to incentivize it. So our main priority in a case like that is to make sure that there is a strong law enforcement response to it to increase the price for perpetrating. And so that it is actually treated like the law says it should be—as a grievous offense to the state."

A Challenging Question

I had spent an entire day talking with the amazing team at IJM, and I left their offices with a greater appreciation for the freedoms I enjoy. I live in a country where I have a voice. And my day of conversations with IJM staff members helped me focus on the essential question: What am I going to do with that voice?

And what are *you* going to do with *your* voice?

GLOBAL PROBLEM IN OUR BACKYARDS

The issues of modern-day slavery and human trafficking aren't limited to developing nations or certain regions of the world. Some of these things happen right here in the United States, including both sex slavery and forced labor.

My wife's uncle recently shared a story with me about a woman he met in South Beach, the ritzy and elite neighborhood of Miami Beach. (Depending on your age, think either the Kardashians or *Miami Vice*.) She was brought to the United States by a wealthy family that lives in Miami, and although they told her she was coming as an indentured servant who could work off the debt of travel expenses by being their housekeeper, she soon found out that she had been duped.

Just like slaves in other nations, she was forced to work for little pay and was unable to get ahead. The family she worked for treated her like a slave and didn't want her to sleep in the house with them. Instead of providing a room for their housekeeper, they put a mattress on the porch and forced her to live outside in the elements.

One day, she finally became brave enough to run away. She happened to run into my uncle-in-law on South Beach, and since then, he and his church have helped her rebuild her life.

Human trafficking and slavery are global issues, and if we are going to fight for the rights of individuals around the world, we can't forget about our neighbors in the United States.

Now that you know more about the problem, let's get back to the Ten Days Without Speech experiment.

STORIES FROM OTHER ADVENTURERS

Frustration!

That was one of my most frequent emotions during my ten days without speech. I'm talking about the kind of frustration that makes my head boil and sends a rush of adrenaline to my heart and hands. The kind that gets my heart beating fast, my arms shaking, and my body feeling like I'm ready to explode. Did someone just harm my family or me and cause me to want revenge? Or was I frustrated because my boss or a coworker treated me unfairly?

Nope.

I got frustrated because people said things I didn't agree with, but I couldn't write fast enough to defend my point of view!

Ever tried having a debate with someone via whiteboard? (If you have, please let me know—we can swap war stories!) I got in maybe one word for every fifteen sentences they spoke. I had so many things to say, and I so desperately wanted to defend my views, but I just couldn't—not without breaking my commitment to go ten days without speech.

But frustration wasn't the only emotion I felt during my ten days without speech, and others who have done the challenge have gone through the emotional gauntlet too.

Rachel, a teenager from Iowa, felt annoyed. "I started realizing how annoying some people who could talk were."

Jason, a pastor in Iowa who participated in Ten Days Without Speech with his youth group, told me that he felt lonely and explained why: "I've noticed that not much talking goes on in my home when I'm around. I think by the time I get home [from work], everyone has filled their quota of words for the day, or they are all introverted nerds with their noses buried in their books. I believe I help balance that equation. As an extrovert who isn't talking, I feel alone. Is this the feeling others sense who are living [in] a world where no one is listening? Or worse, have no voice?"

Some people even faced the feeling of failure! Jason, the Iowa pastor, shared this story:

I had just finished my morning run in front of our neighbor's house, a common occurrence. I was met by the wonderful aroma of bacon. *Hmm, the Kennedys (our neighbors) must be having breakfast!* I thought as I ran past their house to mine. When I entered the back door of my home, I discovered that the bacon smell was actually coming from *our* kitchen.

Without thinking, I exclaimed, "I could smell that fifty feet away!"

My wife, Tamara, shocked and amazed that she heard

me talking, shouted back, "You're not supposed to be talking!"

"Oh no!" I said in horror.

To which she replied, "Bacon made you talk!"

Yup. I blame the bacon.

Riding Through the Rain

On my last day of the experiment, I wanted to fail on purpose—but I didn't give in to temptation. And not being able to use my voice meant being unable to ask for a ride on a rainy afternoon.

There are many days when I leave from work on my bike, tempting a pending thunderhead to erupt into a thunderstorm on my way home. On this particular day, it happened. I rode for over thirty minutes in cool, damp rainwater—the kind your grandmother warns will give you pneumonia. And on top of that, it was a mostly uphill ride home.

Part of me wanted to stop and call Rebecca to pick me up. It started sprinkling about ten minutes into my ride, and I saw the wall of water coming. I easily could have found shelter and waited for her to come pick me up, but I couldn't use my voice. I could have texted her, but she often forgets to check her phone. So instead of sending out an SOS, I kept riding even as the rain became heavier and heavier.

By the time I finally got home, I was absolutely drenched. My wife, in her very supporting and loving tone, laughed until she cried. My boys came to witness the nonsense. I didn't even bother to walk under the porch roof; I just stood there in the still-pouring rain and laughed with my family.

Not being able to use my voice was very limiting. I hated it.

But I also learned, with great clarity, the power of having a voice. I think Greg, another teenager from Iowa, described this best: "I don't think I can make it. It's too hard, and I can't talk to my friends. My sister and I talked once in a while on accident, but I wanted to cry every time my friends asked me questions. Two bullies were bullying me and my friends, and I wanted to say a snappy comeback—but I couldn't."

I was impressed that Greg kept his mouth shut when he was bullied, but what a potent picture of what it means to have your voice taken from you. What a clear example of how our voices equal power.

TIME FOR ACTION

When I started Ten Days Without Speech, I set a goal of raising $325 to fight slavery. The idea of not speaking was a silly idea in a short time frame, but my goal could pay for a high-caliber IJM lawyer to represent a family in Kenya. And God didn't let my small goal get in the way. God took my loaves and fish, and using IJM's nifty fund-raising tool called FreedomMaker,[24] I brought in $2,030.77 over ten days. I couldn't believe it!

I'm convinced you can have similar reasons to rejoice as you go ten days without speech. Yes, it's a tremendous sacrifice that will require creativity and patience and lots of work for your hand-writing muscles!

Identify the Organization

Clearly, I would strongly recommend partnering with International Justice Mission because of their worthwhile efforts to help victims of modern-day slavery and human trafficking around the world. But plenty of other organizations are involved in this important cause too, and you may not have to look very far to find them. An increasing number of nonprofit organizations and interagency task forces are popping up around the country. Do some research to find out what's already being done in your community, and team up for greater impact! If you want some help picking a partner organization, visit 10dayswithout.com and click on "Partner Organizations" for a few recommendations.

Spread the Word

Tell people what you're doing—and why you're doing it. Talk about it on social media, send out e-mails or letters, and let your friends, family, coworkers, and acquaintances know how they can get involved in the cause. And be sure to invest in a small whiteboard and dry-erase pens so you can keep sharing the message once your ten days begin!

Raise the Funds

Set a small goal, or choose an audacious one. God's in the business of doing the miraculous, so do your part to tell others about your cause and how their financial investment can literally change the life of someone ensnared by modern-day slavery. This isn't about manipulating emotions to rake in the cash; it's about engaging people in a life-changing cause that follows God's command from

Micah 6:8: "To act justly and to love mercy and to walk humbly with your God." Motivate your personal platform to sponsor your experiment by donating a certain amount of cash. People could donate an amount based on each day that you go without speaking (like five dollars a day or fifty dollars a day). Or they could donate an entire sum of cash.

USING YOUR VOICE FOR GOOD—AND FOR GOD

That day I visited International Justice Mission, I used the DC metro system, and as I looked around, I noticed people on smartphones with earbuds in their ears and people reading real and virtual books. Almost everyone on the train was nicely dressed, and the smell of perfume and aftershave mixed with the murky smell of subway tunnels.

When Jesus lived, none of this existed. When the Bible was written, smartphones and subways and digital technology weren't even dreams in anyone's wildest imagination. That led me to a thought: *How does biblical truth apply today to* these *people in* this *world?*

And as I stood on the platform at my final stop, I continued to look around—watching the people eagerly anticipating their ride—and another thought occurred to me: *I didn't know slavery existed, and I wonder if any of these people even know that slavery exists.* Now *that's* something I can help change.

What are you going to use your voice to accomplish? If a voice equals power and influence, and if God can use my small blog to bring in more than $2,000 to fight injustice, think about what God can do through you!

Try it. Go one day, three days, or ten days without speech, and see if you walk away with the same conclusion I did: a voice equals power, and when given the right space, it can make a big impact.

As one of the IJM staff members told me, "This is tough stuff, but remember, it's also full of hope."

9

Don't Ignore Me

Ten Days Without Human Touch to Address Orphans, Widows, Prisoners, and Other Untouchables

➤ ➤ ➤ Religion that God our Father accepts as pure and
faultless is this: to look after orphans and widows
in their distress and to keep oneself from being
polluted by the world.

JAMES 1:27

My name is Daniel Day, and I'm going ten days without human
touch to bring positive human affection to orphans, widows, and
prisoners around the world. For the next ten days I will not be touching anyone. Ten days. No touch. Starts now.

Day 5…There's a day in every parent's life that we look
forward to for a long time. It's the day our son or daughter
says "dadda" or "momma" for the first time. Today, my
one-year-old said for the first time ever, "'addy!"

Really, Finley? On the first day I can't pick you up and
go crazy because you say my name, you're going to look at

me with your big, marble-blue eyes, point with your little finger, and say, "'addy!" Come on, man—not cool!

It has been an amazingly hard day. Amazing because my son called my name for the first time, and hard because I can't pick him up, kiss his face, and dance around the living room with him for saying it. Affectionate human touch is something that many of us take for granted—not necessarily at the beginning of a relationship, but over time it can become something that we expect and get used to.

I remember the first time that I held hands with my high school sweetheart. I was driving a 1998 green Jeep Cherokee Sport on our way home from church youth group. We hadn't been dating long, and I loved the way it felt to have her fingers intertwined with mine. I loved it so much, that I ended up running off the road several different times and ran a stop sign—oops!

Even though I still love the way Rebecca's hands feel in mine, it doesn't quite have the same newness to it that it did in our teens. Not because holding hands isn't special, but because we are used to it and don't think twice about grabbing each other's hand in the car, at the store, or sitting around the house. Instead of a sign of newness and adventure, handholding has become a sign of permanence and commitment.

I won't be taking it for granted this week. For the next ten days I won't be holding hands with my wife. It's not

the only affectionate touch I will miss. I'll miss the way my
boys reach up to me when I get home from work, I'll miss
the way they cuddle up to me when I read them a book,
and I bet I will even miss handshakes at the office. Affectionate and positive human touch is important and a
source of life-giving energy for all of us. Even though ten
days is a short time-span in the grand scheme of someone's
life, it's still going to be difficult.

But think about the people who never get affectionate
human interaction. If going ten days without touch can
help provide positive affections for them, it's all worth it.

When someone says the word *untouchable,* what comes to
mind? I think of the fastest running backs in the National Football League or elite track stars in the Olympics—athletes who
make all other athletes look slow and wimpy. I think of people
with amazing wit and knowledge, whose expertise makes everyone else look like a bunch of uneducated simpletons. In my mind,
the word *untouchable* is a label for the type of elite human being
we all strive to become.

But there is another group of "untouchables" in our world—
in fact, many groups of people. Orphans. Prisoners. Widows.
People living in nursing homes. Kids without dads (or worse, with
abusive dads). Some of these people are deemed untouchable because we purposefully avoid them; others because we forget they
exist. Either way, they don't receive adequate positive human affection, but you and I can change that.

THE POWER OF HUMAN AFFECTION

One of the most powerful moments in the Gospels comes in Matthew 8, when Jesus touched a leprous man. At that time, people with leprosy were untouchables. They had to walk around yelling out "Unclean!" to ensure that a healthy person wouldn't bump into them and contract the disease. Lepers lived in communities outside of town and were removed from their friends, families, and places of worship.

So right after Jesus delivered his beloved Sermon on the Mount, he was surrounded by crowds of people—and out of the throngs came a leprous man who asked to be healed. Although Jesus could've healed this man with a word, he did the unthinkable instead—he touched him and healed him. What a beautiful picture of love.

That encounter illustrates why I went ten days without touch and why it will rock your world too. The experience wakes us up to the people in our world and the people around us every day who just need some positive human affection. Someone to reach out to them and shake their hands. Someone to give them hugs. Someone to show them that they are loved and known and valued.

Ten Days Without Touch is about encouraging action, such as serving at a house for abused women and children, volunteering to serve orphans for a summer, adopting a child who is sitting in an orphanage just miles from your home, or visiting prisoners and looking them straight in the eyes. Look for opportunities to serve people who don't normally get served. Look for the students at your school or the coworkers at your office who seem friendless.

Your simple gesture of a high-five could be one of the most powerful things you could do for a person who feels like no one in the world cares. Be the antibully—the person who makes it a point to care about everyone, instead of being the person deciding who's in and who's out. And put yourself out there.

THE CHALLENGE OF GOING WITHOUT TOUCH

Going without human touch was as difficult as I had anticipated, and it was most problematic at home. My wife graciously went along with my experiment, even though she deeply missed holding hands and kissing and cuddling. But my boys were too young to understand how I could go ten minutes without a hug or a high-five, let alone ten days! I didn't want to raise money for orphans by treating my kids like some, so with the help of my blog followers, I came up with some reasonable exceptions.

In the morning I could give each of my kids a hug and a kiss good-bye when I left for work. At night I could cuddle with them while we read a bedtime book and give them a hug and a kiss good night. Those were the only exceptions I made—for the rest of the time I didn't touch anyone, including my wife.

Daily Demonstrations of Care

What are some of the ways you give and receive affection each day? How many times do you and a loved one hold hands or kiss or embrace? How many hands do you shake? How many high-fives do you give? When you go ten days without touch, each one of those moments is a reminder of all the times you demonstrate love and concern and friendship through meaningful touch. I noticed it whenever I had to refuse a handshake, pulled back after I went to grab my wife's hand, or almost bumped into someone in the store.

Justin, a teenager from Iowa who did several of the Ten Days Without challenges, described three moments when he noticed the same thing:

> The first tough situation I faced today was the home
> football game I went to. The stands are always packed,
> and senior night tonight was no different. Luckily, the
> weather wasn't the greatest, and lots of people cleared
> out at halftime. This made being at the game a little
> easier.
>
> The second situation that was tough was my family
> coming into town. They live pretty far away, so I don't get
> to see them very often. The temptation to give hugs was
> great, but I was able to resist. The last situation that made
> today tough was game five of the National League
> Division Series. In case you weren't aware, the St. Louis
> Cardinals had one of the most amazing clutch wins ever in
> the ninth inning tonight. As I freaked out in the middle of
> my living room, I couldn't give any high fives. I couldn't
> give any pats on the back. And I couldn't give any hugs.
> This was extremely difficult.

Fittingly, the best person to explain Ten Days Without Touch ended up being my two-year-old. I posted a video on my blog where he described the problem. I asked him, "Noah, why is Daddy going ten days without touch?" and he said, "'Cause the boys and girls don't have mommies and daddies to love on them and kiss them and hug them."

Wow. So powerful.

Loving the Least of These

My son's statement really *does* summarize what this challenge is all about—and its core truth is reflected in the words of Jesus found in a remarkable passage of Scripture:

> When the Son of Man comes in his glory, and all the angels with him, he will sit on his throne in heavenly glory. All the nations will be gathered before him, and he will separate the people one from another as a shepherd separates the sheep from the goats. He will put the sheep on his right and the goats on his left.
>
> Then the King will say to those on his right, "Come, you who are blessed by my Father; take your inheritance, the kingdom prepared for you since the creation of the world. For I was hungry and you gave me something to eat, I was thirsty and you gave me something to drink, I was a stranger and you invited me in, I needed clothes and you clothed me, I was sick and you looked after me, I was in prison and you came to visit me."
>
> Then the righteous will answer him, "Lord, when did we see you hungry and feed you, or thirsty and give you something to drink? When did we see you a stranger and

invite you in, or needing clothes and clothe you? When did we see you sick or in prison and go to visit you?"

The King will reply, "I tell you the truth, whatever you did for one of the least of these brothers of mine, you did for me."

Then he will say to those on his left, "Depart from me, you who are cursed, into the eternal fire prepared for the devil and his angels. For I was hungry and you gave me nothing to eat, I was thirsty and you gave me nothing to drink, I was a stranger and you did not invite me in, I needed clothes and you did not clothe me, I was sick and in prison and you did not look after me."

They also will answer, "Lord, when did we see you hungry or thirsty or a stranger or needing clothes or sick or in prison, and did not help you?"

He will reply, "I tell you the truth, whatever you did not do for one of the least of these, you did not do for me."

Then they will go away to eternal punishment, but the righteous to eternal life. (Matthew 25:31–46)

God used these verses to reveal an important truth in my life: I didn't care about the "untouchables" whom Jesus cared about—specifically prisoners. When I read this passage, I knew that I needed to confront my unchristian bias and prejudice toward prisoners. I needed to die to myself. And I found out that by dying to myself, I gave myself the opportunity to really live.

As you read those words just now, maybe God didn't speak to you about prisoners but about a different group of people who are ignored or rejected or forgotten. You want to help widows or shut-ins or the elderly. Or you want to serve the hungry and thirsty who have become society's outcasts. Or you want to spend time with the sick, AIDS victims, or people suffering from life-threatening illnesses.

Because that biblical passage resonates differently with each of us, I wanted to help people consider a variety of ways to help the untouchables in today's world. If they felt God speaking to them about orphans, they could donate to an organization such as Livada Orphan Care—a ministry to orphans in Romania. Or they could connect with Prison Fellowship and visit prisoners. Or they could go to a local nursing home and visit the elderly. Or they could find a local home for single moms and children, such as Family Life Services, and play with kids.

Each of these is a group deemed untouchable, one of the least of these. Each of these is a group of people whose lives will be changed as you reach out, serve, support, and touch.

Orphans: So in Need of Love

Orphans are victims of circumstances—people whom we may care about but don't typically come into contact with. If you asked most people if they care about orphans, they would say yes. But if you then asked what they're doing to help orphans, they could point to nothing specific.

My first encounter with orphans came in Romania many years ago, when I was an eighteen-year-old from North Carolina who didn't know what to expect. The orphanage we visited was shaped like a hotel, but the grounds were poorly kept: weeds crawled up the side of the building and poked through the gravel driveway, long wispy grass grew out of place in flower beds and on the playground, and the building itself was ghostly barren. Everything—from the iron gate at the entrance to the concrete walls—gave off a sense of coldness that sent chills up my spine. *How could anyone live here?* I thought.

I began to imagine that the building was full of buzzing fluorescent lights and staffed by men with greenish skin and white lab coats. (Clearly I've watched far too many creepy movies!) But when our van pulled into the parking lot, the building came to life as smiling kids bubbled out of every crack and crevice.

As I stepped out of the van, I immediately was pulled in several different directions by little boys and girls. A boy around five years old grabbed my hand and started pulling me toward the front door. His black hair, olive skin, and big brown eyes convinced me to follow—confident that this kid's smile could light up even the darkest building. As he jerked me forward toward the door, I grabbed one of our interpreters and dragged him along for the ride.

Heartbreaking Conditions

When we walked through the front door, I noticed an odor mixed with the cold, damp air of the orphanage. It smelled old and musty and got stronger with each passing step. Soon the smell was overwhelming, and I started to feel sick. I never got used to that smell.

Sadly, the orphanage was just as gloomy, barren, and depressing on the inside as it was on the outside. The ancient yellow tile was stained by years of foot traffic by children who never had parents to teach them to wipe their shoes at the door. The walkway from the entrance was like a handicap ramp and gradually descended into the heart of the building. The walkway cut between two raised platforms. On the right-hand side, four teenagers were playing Ping-Pong on an old table with a droopy net. And on the left, a few adults sat around a table—ignoring us, just as they ignored the children. My five-year-old tour guide pulled me forward, and we walked up a flight of concrete stairs.

His room was on the second floor, and the closer he got to it, the more his pride showed. He was proud of his setup and wanted us to see everything that was special to him. He showed us his dirty bed covered in a dirty red blanket. He showed us a greasy black stuffed animal, which he kept hidden so no one would steal it. He showed us his nearly empty drawer of dirty clothes.

"Doesn't he have any nice clothes or a clean toy?" I asked our translator. "Don't they receive donations?"

"There are a lot of toys and clothes that get donated to the orphanages in Romania, but it's pretty much common practice for the caretakers to go through it first and take home the best stuff for their own kids."

Part of me was sad for the orphans. Another part of me got mad.

But my anger faded as the infectious joy of my five-year-old tour guide penetrated my heart. Somehow, he was still thankful for his limited possessions. His smile felt so out of place—seemingly the only bit of happiness and life in the entire building.

As we turned to leave the room, I noticed a few locks on the doors. "Wow," I said to the translator, "it's almost like a prison!"

"Those locks are important," he explained. "Older boys, especially, prey on the younger boys and girls. It's not uncommon for boys like that five-year-old holding your hand to be raped—in fact, he may have already been sexually molested. Some of the girls get raped as well, but often they give up themselves willingly. When they don't get any kind of love and affection, sex is at least something."

I didn't say a word. What *could* I have said? My heart was broken.

Outcasts from Another Orphanage

As we walked away, I heard loud music coming from one of the larger rooms downstairs. Curious, I walked into an empty room that didn't feel like a part of an orphanage—cavernous, cold, damp, and loud, like a medieval ballroom minus the tapestries and roaring fires. Inside the room I found several unkempt girls lined up against a concrete wall, rocking back and forth. Next to the girls on the carpetless concrete floor sat a radio playing obnoxiously loud Gypsy music.

"What is this?" I asked the interpreter.

"These girls are not originally from this orphanage," he said. "They are from a different institution that shut down. When it closed, thirty-five girls with special needs were dropped into this orphanage because there wasn't anywhere else for them to go. Unfortunately, the caretakers don't have any training in mental disabilities, and they view these girls as 'in the way' and a 'nuisance.'

So their solution is to turn on loud Gypsy music for the girls every day and hide them in this room by themselves."

That was the straw that broke my tear ducts wide open. Tears began to fill my eyes as I walked over to the girls. The closer I got, the more I saw signs of very apparent mental and physical disabilities. One girl in particular looked at me with a distrustful look.

"Can I approach them?" I asked, sensing that most of these girls were apprehensive to my presence.

"Yes, but be gentle," he responded. "Most of these girls have been raped numerous times."

I slowly went down the line and made it a point to hug each girl. Through the translator, I told each of them that they were loved and that someone cared about them.

I will never forget those girls. I will never forget how hopeless I felt. I will never forget how angry I was, yet there was nothing I could do about it. These precious girls were alone, cut off from the rest of the children. More importantly, they were cut off from any love and positive affection—yet all I could do was give them hugs and tell them that I loved them.

When we got back in the van to leave, my mind was consumed with questions. *How would a quick hug make a lasting difference? How could a brief moment of love provide the special care and attention that these girls would need for the rest of their lives?*

Obviously not every orphanage in the world features such dire conditions or children from such troubling situations. But every orphanage—whether here in our country or in another nation—is home to children who deserve a family, a place to call home. And many are home to children who have been abandoned, neglected, and abused.

Inasmuch as we love and serve and adopt the orphans, we do it unto Jesus.

ABUSED WOMEN AND CHILDREN: VICTIMS OF HURTFUL TOUCH

Orphans aren't the only group of "untouchables" who desperately need positive affection and love. There are older people within nursing homes and communities who never receive visitors. I have met prisoners who told me that their families want nothing to do with them. And I have met people who are homeless, never see their families, and don't know where their own children live.

Most of us care; we just don't make an effort to serve these groups of people.

During my Ten Days Without Touch experiment, I researched local homes that assist abused women and children. The online search results included a well-respected organization that I had helped in the past but had forgotten about because of the busyness of life. As I read the description of Family Life Services, I was reminded that each family lives on campus for a very low fee and has access to counseling, crisis assistance, and life-skills training. Perfect!

Every year, over 3.3 million instances of child abuse in the United States are reported, involving more than 6 million children. In fact, five children die each day because of abuse—most of them are under the age of four.[25] In these situations, positive touch has been replaced by violent and abusive contact. The lack of positive human affection is a problem—and is something God cares about.

I decided to volunteer at the Thursday-night get-together, where the moms go to a small group and all the kids gather for a lesson and games. It was quite an experience, especially when one of the girls brought out her rats—not ugly sewer rats from New York, but pet rats that were supposedly cute. (Sorry, folks, but I didn't get it. I've always been more of a dog guy.)

I love interacting with kids, and girls hold a special place in my heart—probably because I grew up with three younger sisters and because so far God has blessed us with sons. This soft spot backfired that night, though, when a very sweet girl wanted a ride on my shoulders, and I agreed. What I didn't realize was that her offer was a package deal. You know those hidden fees that show up in everything these days? (No, airline companies, I'm not talking about you—well, not *just* you.) It was kind of like that. I did have the great privilege of giving her a ride, but I also got to give her white pet rat a ride too. In fact, she thought it was hilarious to set the rodent on me throughout the rest of the evening.

These fatherless children and their loving mothers were people whom I didn't normally come in contact with. Spending time with them reminded me of how obedience to God often requires us taking deliberate, intentional steps—steps of faith, at times. It's a much better path for us to walk instead of neglecting the people God loves.

Inasmuch as we love and serve and care for women and children who've suffered, we do it unto Jesus.

PRISONERS: NEAR US, YET FAR AWAY

For most of my life, caring about prisoners and prison ministry was never on my radar. Not only did I feel like they deserved to be separated from humanity, but I also lacked mercy or compassion for them—an attitude so far from the heart of Jesus.

But there is an old saying that I took to heart the day that Jesus's words in Matthew 25 rocked my world: "It's never too late to start." Almost immediately after reading that verse in summer 2012, I contacted Jan, a woman who works with Prison Fellowship here in Colorado Springs, and told her that I needed to go into a prison. I had been intentionally avoiding prisoners—they were a group of untouchables in my life—but if I was going to live and be like Jesus, things needed to change. She agreed to set something up for me.

A few weeks later, I arrived at Jan's house at 6:30 a.m. sharp, and although I missed breakfast, I felt good knowing I was on time. Her husband warmly welcomed me into the house and told me to have a seat while Jan finished getting ready. A few minutes later, she walked downstairs and greeted me, and we headed out for our hourlong journey to the prison.

As each mile passed, I became more and more talkative. When I get nervous, I talk, and the closer we got to the prison, the more my mouth sped up. During our conversation, Jan told me that the greatest punishment of prison is removal from love. This surprised me, because I always thought that the punishment of prison was being removed from the world.

"It's not that a prisoner is removed from the world that makes prison hell for them—it's the fact that they are removed from the people that they care about and that care about them," she said. "Trust me, my son was in prison, and I could only give him a hug when I entered and a hug when I left—that was it! It was very painful for him and for me."

Second-Guessing My Visit

As we approached the prison, my eyes noticed a chain-link fence on the horizon. The closer we got to the complex, the more my decision to visit a prison seemed, well, stupid. Off to the left a huge gray concrete building with small slit windows rose out from behind a hill. As we pulled up to the gate under the shadow of this monstrous cavern surrounded by razor-sharp barbed wire, my fear became palpable. My hands shook as I pulled out my driver's license for the guard, and my heart began beating out of my chest as if I had just finished eight cups of highly caffeinated coffee.

The guard was a lot nicer than I expected him to be. I was imagining one of the beefy guys with a bad attitude I had seen on TV shows, but he was normal and even told a joke. But I didn't hear his humor—my eyes were fixed on the multistory concrete structure on the left.

I felt relieved when we drove past the entrance to the huge concrete maximum-security prison—and didn't go in.

"So that's not where we're going?" I asked in a relieved tone.

"No, there are actually seven prisons on this property, and we are going to the one up there on the hill."

My eyes followed the road up the hill to a small set of buildings at the peak. Although surrounded by razor-sharp barbed

wire, the buildings looked far less daunting than the concrete behemoth we had passed. As we pulled into the parking lot, some of
my fear began to fade. I was still anxious about interacting with
inmates, but I was also curious to see what life was like on the
other side of the fence.

Inside the Gates of a Prison

We walked up to the gate, and I got a look at the barbed wire. I
had grown up on a small hay farm and knew the rural barbed wire
that keeps cows from wandering away from home. As a kid, I was
really good at climbing over barbed-wire fences without snagging
my clothes or my skin. But the prison barbed wire was different.
As I stared up at the rolls of razor blades that lined the top of the
thick chain-link fence, I knew there was no climbing over that
one. And I found out from the guard that pigeons often got stuck
on the razor-sharp barbs—not a pleasant sight!

As the guard processed our IDs and gave us visitor passes, I
looked around at the complex. For the first time in my life I was
standing on the inside of a prison yard. My view of the Rocky
Mountains was broken up through the links of the fence. I love to
hike and can't imagine what it would be like to stare at the mountains every day without the freedom to go climb them. Then another thought hit me, *I haven't been hiking in months.* Just think,
I have the freedom to enjoy creation, and yet I don't take advan-
tage of it—and I was about to meet men who had lost that privilege for a period of time.

When we came around the guardhouse, the complex opened
up into a giant courtyard, with exercise equipment right in the mid-

dle. It looked like Venice Beach in Los Angeles, with guys pulling down on pulleys attached to large stacks of black weights, out in the open for all to see. A few months earlier, my wife and I had visited LA for the first time, and we were entertained watching very strong guys lifting weights outside in Venice Beach—probably to impress the ladies. (I had considered joining in but didn't want to embarrass any of the locals!) It was a fascinating contrast that at Venice Beach, guys were lifting weights as an exercise of their freedom—yet in the prison, guys were lifting weights to distract themselves from the fact that they didn't have freedom.

The room we met in looked like a normal classroom that you could find in any high school around the country. Instead of individual desks, the inmates sat behind tables pushed together to make a U-shape around the edge of the room, with another smaller row of desks in the middle. Just like most classes that I attended in high school and college, the outside seats were taken first. I was surprised to find that the entire room filled up.

Confronting My Own Selfishness

The group included a diverse mix of men: white guys, black guys, a Vietnamese immigrant, a Native American, guys with big muscles, ones with small muscles, some with big beards and others clean shaven, many with tattoos, and some wearing glasses. Even their prison terms were diverse. I met a guy who had spent thirty-five years in prison and another who'd been there for five. Some of them had been in the maximum-security units like the one I had seen on the way in, and others had spent their time in minimum-security prisons like the one we were in that day.

The only things these twenty-one men had in common were the standard-issue forest-green jumpsuit—and the fact that they had all made some kind of mistake or bad choice that had landed them behind bars. They were also a part of Prison Fellowship's Transformational Program to help them get out and stay out of prison for the rest of their lives.

"Good morning, everyone," Jan began.

"Good morning, Jan!" the men responded enthusiastically.

"Today we have a special guest with us. Daniel and I sat down for coffee the other day, and I was so excited to hear his heart and hear about what the Lord is teaching him. He is looking for guys who are willing to help him understand what prison is really like and to hear from some of you about your stories and experiences. If you don't feel comfortable sharing, please feel free to just listen. But I know this is a transparent group, so I figure that won't be many of you!"

As I heard Jan introducing me, I was suddenly confronted by my own selfishness. Here I was, hanging out with twenty-one guys whom I had spent my life avoiding. Twenty-one guys whom God said he cared about, but I didn't. Even more powerfully, I was confronted by the fact that I wasn't here to invest in the lives of these guys; I was here for personal development—an experiment of sorts. I was here to check off another command on the spiritual checklist of Christianity so that I could feel better about saying that I'm a Christ follower. As Jan began to wind down her introduction, my hidden agenda was at the forefront of my mind.

Going Because Jesus Says to Go

As I began to speak, I couldn't help but begin by confessing to these guys why I was really here. I told them about how I had been reading Matthew 25 and felt challenged by the words of Jesus, that he "was in prison and you came to visit me." God was teaching me that I had this massive blind spot in my life, and I needed to respond.

"Not only have I never been in a prison before today," I told the men, "but in the past I have never even cared to go into a prison. I've never cared about guys like you before. But I'm here today because Jesus says to go, and I'm excited to get to know you and learn more about what prison life is like."

I told the men about a woman I'd spoken with a few days earlier. When she heard that I was going to visit some inmates, she basically said prisoners deserved to be in prison and didn't deserve any special attention. They should work for their food and be separated from society because of the severity of their mistakes. And I admitted that I'd held similar attitudes in the past.

"But I'm also here because the organization that I work for spends a lot of time speaking to kids who have grown up in Christian homes, Christian schools, and Christian churches—just like I did," I added. "What can you say to them to help them understand why Jesus cares about prisoners?"

A guy raised his hand. "I also grew up in a Christian school, home, and church," he said. "I was just like that girl you talked to and those kids that you will speak with each year. I had hopes and dreams just like they do. I remember my dad asked me at six years old what I wanted to be when I grew up, and I told him that I wanted to be just like him. We laughed and kept doing whatever it was that we were doing. I just say that to say that we are all one bad decision away from getting in here. Do we deserve to be here? Yeah, we do. But I would just remind people that we have all fallen short."

Another guy jumped in: "I just wanted to add to his thoughts. Doesn't the Bible say that we have all fallen short of the glory of God? Doesn't it say that we have all sinned? I don't think it distinguishes between prisoners and regular people when it talks about violating God's laws."

This same idea echoed around the room for several minutes as different guys took turns nodding, reading Scripture, and putting in their two cents about humanity's depravity. Several men also talked about how much Jesus has done for them.

Change Begins with Hope

"We all deserve to be here, and I don't want you to think that we are sitting here thinking that we deserve to be free," one of the guys said. "We all made mistakes. You are talking about changing people's perspectives on the outside—well, you can't change those perspectives. It's not your job. It's *our* job as felons to change people's perspectives. The reason people on the outside who have never been to prison have that perspective on inmates is because we keep stepping on people. I've been out a couple of times, and every time someone gives me a chance, I end up stepping on them by stealing their car or getting their daughter pregnant. It's all of our faults that the perception exists, and it's our job to change that when we get out."

"Well, how do you do that?" I asked. "How do you get out and stay out?"

"Change begins with real hope," one of the men said. "That hope is definitely centered in faith in Jesus, but that faith isn't enough on its own for us prisoners. After faith we need to find purpose—and for me that comes through the Holy Spirit. Then I need someone to believe in me. When I have those three things, I begin to find hope.

"We have guys come in all of the time and yell at us to 'turn or burn.' But that's not hope. Hope is when a pastor comes in and tells me the truth about Jesus but then looks me in the eye and says, 'I want to see your face in our church family photo book. You need to get on your best behavior and get out of here so you can come be a part of our community and family. Did you hear me? The next mug shot you get better be the one that we take and that ends up in our church directory!' Those are the pastors that bring hope. They actually believe in the redemption that they teach—to the point that they are willing to let us join their church when we get out."

Amens echoed throughout the room. It was powerful to see a group of prisoners agree that they needed someone to believe in them, to spend time with them, and to invest in their lives. It continued to reinforce the conviction of Matthew 25 that God began placing in my heart over a week earlier.

The Power of a Personal Visit

It was time to end, but I had to ask one more question: "How important is it for people to come visit you?"

"That lady right there, Jan, has made the difference in my life," said another man, tears welling up in his eyes. "I've been in and out of prison my entire life, and I've never had anyone care for me the way she does. She not only brought hope but also love. Thanks to her, I have the confidence to finally get out and stay out."

"He's right," said another inmate. "Jan made the difference in my life too, and now thanks to Transformational Ministries [the in-prison ministry of Prison Fellowship], I have a mentor who will be working with me in here and when I get out of here. The other day I met my mentor for the first time. Now, I don't get visited much in prison just because my family lives out of state, and let's face it—it's not a very popular thing to hang out with inmates. So when I found out that I had a mentor and that he was coming to the prison to meet with me, I couldn't wait. My hands were shaking because I was so excited to have someone who cared about me and because of the time he spent with me—for the first time I really knew I could change and be different. It's not just the accountability; it's the fact that someone cares enough on the outside to come on the inside and invest in my life."

As I shook hands with the different inmates, I was blown away by their joy and gratitude. They were so thankful that I had come. I felt guilty as I walked out of the prison because it seemed like I had received a lot more than I had given them.

I won't forget those guys. They are responsible for a major paradigm shift in my life from a prejudiced holier-than-thou attitude to a compassionate desire to help guys get their feet under them. Several of them had said, "All that we need is a hand-up—not a handout, but a hand-up." I think I can do that—I think we can all do that.

Is God calling you to be a Jan? Is God calling you to be a pastor or a leader who delivers hope behind prison walls? Is God calling you to be a mentor?

Inasmuch as we love and serve and care for the prisoners, we do it unto Jesus.

TIME FOR ACTION

So how can you make a difference in the lives of "untouchables"? You've probably picked up a lot of ideas already in this chapter, but here are some additional thoughts:

Begin with Prayer

Prayer should always be our foundation as we seek to serve others, but I believe it's especially essential for the Ten Days Without Touch challenge. What is God calling *you* to do? That answer will be different from the answer I got or the answers others might get. Reread that passage from Matthew 25, and ask God to reveal how you can serve the least of these—and to help you see which group you can best reach.

Find an Organization

Start in your own backyard. (Well, not your actual backyard—you know what I mean.) Once you know how God wants you to serve, research the ministries and organizations committed to that cause. See if their involvement aligns with your passion, and discuss specific opportunities for service and involvement.

Inform and Recruit People

One of the beauties of this challenge is that you have opportunities to serve here in this country *and* in other nations. You may be able to use your ten days without human touch to raise funds for overseas ministries, or you might be able to focus on specific ways people can serve in your community. You don't have to travel far to find orphans, prisoners, and families in need. But if you join a group on an overseas mission trip, you will find them there too. And the experience—whether at home or abroad—becomes even richer when you bring along family and friends for the adventure.

BREAKING THE RULES

Earlier in this chapter I said I didn't touch anyone except during those morning and evening interactions with my boys. That isn't entirely accurate. Let me explain.

Toward the end of my challenge I came home from work early one day—a day when my wife had nearly reached the breaking point because of caring for our two boys plus one of Noah's friends. That means that while I was putting in long hours at the office, she was putting in long hours with one-, two-, and three-year-old boys. For those of you who don't have any boys or have never watched boys, let me explain to you what she was going through—and I'll use Rebecca's description:

"Excuse me, Noah—look at me in the eyes, you need to learn how to share. You were not using that toy."

"Caed, please climb down off of the entertainment center."

"Where's Finley?" (Evil laughter coming from the stairs.)

"Stop fighting!"

"Give me that shovel! This is not a toy—don't touch it again!"

"No one touch anyone with anything for the rest of the day!"

"Noah and Caed, why are you two naked? Put your clothes back on. We don't walk around outside without clothes on."

"Noah, please take the Mr. Potato Head pieces out of your ears."

"Caed, stop putting mud in the pool."

"Noah, we don't push babies!"

"Finley, are you pooping?"

So when I walked in the door on Thursday and heard all this, I knew my lovely wife was having a very hard day. But I made things worse when I opened the fridge and asked, "Why don't we have any food in this house?"

Okay, I'm just going to pause for a moment and let you picture what could have happened next—all the ways my wife could
have reacted and all the things she could have said. Ready? Let's
move on with the story. If you're not married yet, please understand that this was a very, *very* stupid thing to say. (That was
meant for all you guys; you ladies seem to be much wiser about
what to say in these stressful situations.) Fortunately, I married a
loving, merciful woman, so she didn't say all the things she could
have said—and maybe should have said! But Rebecca needed a
break. She wanted to go out and go shopping, so that's what she
did. That left me with two napping boys and one who was awake.

Within minutes, our one-year-old woke up after only a twenty-
minute nap. His screaming woke up his brother, and I soon realized
what my wife had been dealing with for the past three days.

This was when I failed: from the moment Finley woke up, I
was carrying him around until Rebecca got home. He was screaming, and the only way he was happy was on my hip. But when you
have one-, two-, and three-year-old boys under a roof for more
than five minutes, you gotta do what you gotta do!

And in many ways, that cliché—you gotta do what you gotta
do—is why I went ten days (almost) without touch. What happens if we don't go in and visit prisoners? What happens if we
don't love on children who don't have parents? What happens if
abused moms never have someone who cares about them? What
happens if the widows and elderly are left alone, without a friend
in the world? What happens if we ignore society's outcasts?

We gotta do what we gotta do.

10

Bringing It All Together

> ➤ ➤ ➤ But don't just listen to God's word. You must do
> what it says. Otherwise, you are only fooling
> yourselves.
>
> JAMES 1:22, NLT

It's pretty easy to have a listening faith. The preacher delivers great messages every weekend. Your small-group leader offers some dynamic insights every Tuesday night. All your favorite podcasts convey incredible truths as you drive to work.

But for too many of us, that's it. That's as far as our faith goes. Just as we're consumers of clothing and movies and huge homes and electronic gadgets, we become consumers of all things biblical. Consume, consume, consume—without ever living out the truths we're consuming.

Guess what? God says there's something more to life and to this whole adventure of faith. God calls us to a deeper faith, a more active faith—a faith that's demonstrated through our actions and our lifestyle. Your life was meant for something more!

That's why Ten Days Without has the potential to radically shake up your life. It'll move you from a listening faith to a doing faith, from a faith that absorbs to a faith that serves, from a faith that's self-centered to a faith that's others-centered.

FOLLOW JESUS'S EXAMPLE

One of my favorite passages of Scripture is in Philippians 2, where the apostle Paul encourages his first-century readers—and all of *us* too—to model our lives after Jesus Christ. And when you think about it, there really isn't anyone better to emulate, right? Forget the world-class athletes or topnotch musicians or flavor-of-the-week celebrities. Jesus is the ultimate role model! Check out these words:

> Each of you should look not only to your own interests,
> but also to the interests of others.
> > Your attitude should be the same as that of Christ
> Jesus:

> Who, being in very nature God,
> > did not consider equality with God something to
> > > be grasped,
> but made himself nothing,
> > taking the very nature of a servant,
> > being made in human likeness.
> And being found in appearance as a man,
> > he humbled himself
> > and became obedient to death—even death on a
> > > cross!

Therefore God exalted him to the highest place
    and gave him the name that is above every name,
that at the name of Jesus every knee should bow,
    in heaven and on earth and under the earth,
and every tongue confess that Jesus Christ is Lord,
    to the glory of God the Father.

Therefore, my dear friends, as you have always obeyed—not only in my presence, but now much more in my absence—continue to work out your salvation with fear and trembling, for it is God who works in you to will and to act according to his good purpose. (Philippians 2:4–13)

Let's take a closer look at these verses. Even if you've read them a thousand times or have them memorized, put on a pair of fresh lenses to see how going ten days without will impact your life.

You'll Move from a Self-Centered Faith to an Others-Centered Faith

Have you picked up on this idea as a recurring theme throughout this book? In Philippians 2:4, Paul encourages us to look out for other people's interests and needs, not just our own.

Becoming others-centered isn't easy for me, and I'm guessing it's not easy for you either—partly because of our fallen nature as sinful human beings and partly because we live in a culture that gives lip service to it, while shouting and selling a self-centered lifestyle. That's why going without is so helpful. It causes us to think about the challenges and obstacles other people face. The experience reminds us that a truly Christ-centered faith means looking beyond ourselves and paying attention to the needs in our world—and then doing something to meet those needs.

And when we do this, we'll have a clearer perspective on what matters most and a deeper appreciation for all the ways God has blessed us.

You'll Discover the Rewards of a Humble Lifestyle

Having the attitude of a servant is basically "doing without" in order to serve others—that's what Paul teaches us in Philippians 2:5–9. Doing without is learning to live like Jesus.

Humility is closely aligned to an others-centered attitude. Pride tells us we can do it on our own, but humility reminds us of our need for God. Pride tells us we always need to be right (or at least make other people *think* we're always right), but humility reminds us of our limitations. Pride fuels our selfishness and greed, but humility fuels our love and compassion.

When Jesus came to this earth, it was the ultimate act of humility. Think about it: Jesus, God the Son, became human. He chose to experience the joys and pains, the laughter and tears, the bumps and bruises and cuts and aches that we all endure each day. And then he took that one step further and willingly died on the cross to pay the price for our sins. He sacrificed so we could live. He gave up his life so we could experience abundant life and eternal life. Wow!

Going ten days without requires far less sacrifice, but it gives us a clearer glimpse into the heart of God—and it's all rooted in humility.

You'll Experience New Ways of Worshiping God

Far too many people in our churches have a narrow definition of worship. It goes something like this: "Those songs we sing at the beginning of a church service." And that's it—that's what "worship" means to them.

Is singing a form of worship? Of course! But it's just one way to worship God. When I look at Philippians 2:10–11, I'm drawn toward this understanding of worship: if I'm doing something that points people toward Jesus as Lord or directs glory and honor to God, then it's a form of worship, an act of worship, a demonstration of worship.

And the truest, most powerful worship is demonstrated through actions, not just words. Why? Because words are easy. Actions are difficult. I can tell you I love people who are homeless, but if I never spend time with them, never get to know them as individuals loved by God, never serve them, and never look for ways to help them escape the cycle of poverty, how genuine is my love?

When you go without, you'll more easily embrace serving others as an incredible way to worship God.

You'll Have the Chance to Celebrate Results

At the end of the day, God is the one who changes lives. When you and I go without shoes or speech or furniture, we point the way to God—he's the one who transforms.

As followers of Christ, we have the most incredible gifts: forgiveness of our sins, God's presence each day through his Holy Spirit, and the promise of eternal life with God. If we hold on to that good news and don't share it with others through our actions and our lifestyle, then we aren't fulfilling the mission God has for us.

But when we live out that mission, we get to be part of that transformative journey. We provide resources, we create awareness, we engage volunteers, we spread the message—we do *our* part so God can do *his* part. Why did God create things to work this way? I have no idea! It's on my list of "So God, what were you thinking?" questions that I'll someday ask him. (Why I'm not a famous athlete is on that list too!) All I know is that our life mission centers around God's grace, serving others, and celebrating results in our lives, in our friends' lives, in the organizations we support, and in the people who are served.

LET GOD MESS YOU UP

I'm praying that your life will never be the same after you go ten days without. In fact, I'm praying that God will so challenge and stretch you that you can't go back to living the same way— that God will royally mess you up, in the purest sense of that phrase.

How has this whole adventure messed me up?

I have seen how going without shoes breaks up the rhythm of my day and opens me up to caring about issues I would normally forget about or ignore.

I've learned that I don't have to avoid people who are homeless—I can and should help them in meaningful, significant ways.

I have recognized that I spend *way too much* time consuming media, which causes me to miss out on life, especially in areas where I could make a difference. I've learned I need to spend less time with movies and more with Scripture.

I have a much better understanding of the challenges people face in developing nations, and I experience deeper compassion for them and a greater gratitude for the blessings in my life.

I am beginning to see people just like Jesus sees them—as the handiwork of God. I can be a big help to my friends and family affected by disabilities.

I realize that caring about the environment is about biblical, God-centered stewardship. I don't have to agree with everyone's politics on the issue, but as a steward, I should actively care about the world.

I have met people who never receive positive human affection. Some of these people I had purposely shunned, while others I had avoided because I saw them as "inconvenient." But I can be the person who shows them God's love by being the one to love them.

The lessons go on and on—and I'm not done learning. I don't want to *ever* be done learning what it means to be a more intentional, passionate, devoted, active follower of Christ. I hope that's your desire too. (If you want to see what I'm learning, you can check out my blog at danielryanday.com.)

Let me close with a few final words of encouragement.

Do This as a Team

Amazing things become even more amazing when shared with others. This adventure will be exponentially more rewarding if you get your friends, family members, youth group, small group, neighbors, or church involved.

Do This Soon

You've heard about my adventures of going ten days without. Don't sit around and let these ideas slowly drift into the "good intentions" category. Visit my website (10dayswithout.com) and check out my FAQ page on how to put this book into action right away!

Do This Passionately

Your sacrifice can change lives—literally. Grasp the potential of being able to make a difference in your community or in a village on the other side of the world. Pray that God would fill you with fervent compassion—and with his unending passion for helping those in need.

Do This Often

Once you experience your first Ten Days Without challenge, I pray that you'll get hooked. I pray that you'll do stuff I've never even dreamed of—and that God's name will be glorified for generations to come. Use this adventure as a launching pad for a life filled with others-centered service, and your life will never be the same again. I guarantee it!

Now, let's get out there and go without!

Acknowledgments

Yep. I'm going to do it. I'm going to start by thanking God. I
don't feel obligated to do this. I'm not doing this because I'm
worried about what others will think if I write a book about being
an intentional Christian and don't mention my source of inspiration and clarity. Okay, maybe those factors play in a little bit, but
that's beside the point. The point is that God is my inspiration for
writing this book. Every day during this process I've prayed that
this book would be full of his words, his ideas, and his thoughts.
So thank you, God, for inspiration.

To Rebecca! This book wouldn't exist without you. Literally.
You helped me come up with the concept. You supported me.
Encouraged me. And loved me through the entire process. Thank
you! You're beautiful and amazing, and I'm so honored to be your
husband.

To my boys! Thank you for providing so many great stories!
Without you and your natural inspiration, writing ten blogs over
ten days for each experiment would have been impossible! Without you I would have also finished this book sooner! I love being
your daddy. You are my pride and my joy!

To my mom and dad. My first blog followers! You should
be proud of this book because I am who I am because of you.
You taught me that dreams are possible. Your love for each

other is inspiring and in so many ways taught me about God's love.

To Megan, Eric, Angela, Thandie, Micah, Rina, Drew, Vi, Janelle, and Sam. You are the best siblings a guy could ask for! Thank you for helping me pursue my dreams.

To David and Jeanette Meffen. Thank you for welcoming me into your family and inspiring me with your passion for Jesus.

Abuelo y Abuela. Gracias por la sabiduría qué ustedes han compartido con migo y la inspiración que ustedes me dan.

To Grandma Aldrich. Thank you for encouraging me in my writing, and thank you for constantly loading me up with old books.

To Steve Reed! The first person (besides my mom) to believe in my story and ability as a writer. You helped my dream of becoming an author come true. The *Ten Days Without* book exists because you believed in it. I am so thankful for you!

To David Kopp! Your patience and encouragement gave me so much confidence. Thank you for helping me figure out what I was really writing about—the core of the message. Thank you (and kind-of-sort-of Panera Bread Company) for all the coffee and bagels. I hope you're proud of these pages, because your perseverance helped them come into existence.

To Susan Tjaden, my M&M'S buddy! (I really want to spell something wrong just to make you roll your eyes!) Thank you for your linear brain! You also taught me that editors are the people who turn average M&M'S into dark chocolate M&M'S.

To Rob Cunningham. You gave *Ten Days Without* a chance. Your refinement of the message made this book so much more compelling than I could have made it on my own.

To Axis (i.e., David, Jeremiah, DGiddy, Nicholas, Meghan, Melanie, AJ, Patrick, Amanda, and all of my supporters). Thank you for providing a space for this concept and book to grow and flourish.

To Caed. Somehow you ended up in this book twice! Thank you for the memorable stories!

To Tom Dellinger, Brent Culbertson, Ashley Evans, and Greg Lewallen. You taught me that life is worship. Tom, you gave me a journal and wrote in the front of it, "Daniel. The message 'life is worship' is yours to take to the world." I hope you're proud of this book!

To Jason, Justin, Tamara, Lisa, Katy, Warner, and the rest of the youth from First Assembly of God, Des Moines. Your stories and willingness to try something new made this book *so much better*! Thank you for being a part of this project. I hope you're proud of the result!

To Vianca, Daniel K., Patrick, Daniel G., David, and Brian. Thank you for being a part of this experiment. Thank you for testing the ideas and writing about them.

To Brent, Rachel, Bryce, Lisa, Jenny, and Caroline. Thank you for allowing me to crash the Twin Rocks Joni and Friends Family Retreat! What an amazing and life-changing experience! Bryce and Jenny, you two are my heroes!

To Corey. Your hug at the Special Olympics changed my life.

To Diane, Jessica, and the rest of Joni and Friends. Thank you! I'm so proud to represent Joni and Friends in this book.

To Lori, Christa, Saju, Philip, Blair, and the entire IJM staff. Thank you for teaching me about slavery and injustice in the world. Your stories and expertise were enlightening and challenging. Thank you for being a beacon of justice in a dark world. Thank you, Christa, for reminding me that fighting slavery is a story of hope and a future—not darkness!

To Jan, Prison Fellowship, and all the guys behind bars who were willing to share their stories with me. Thank you for challenging me to grow up in my faith.

To Tim and Compassion International. *Wow!* Honduras was heartbreaking and amazing. I hope everyone sponsors a child! Thank you for helping me understand poverty a little more!

To Bruce and the entire Livada Orphan Care staff. Thank you for the most amazing internship and experience of my life! May God bless your orphan ministry in Romania.

To Rita Johnson and the rest of the SHUZZ team. Thank you for jumping on board with a random guy from Colorado! Your quick response and enthusiasm gave *Ten Days Without* the push it needed to become a reality.

To Ms. Williams, Mrs. Goffin, Mrs. Frost, Mrs. Davis, and the rest of the Asheville Christian Academy faculty and staff. You know why you're mentioned here. Susan, your patience with my bad grammar (and my personality) paved the way for me to become an author. JoLynn, your love for stories—real stories— inspired me to pursue writing. Mrs. Frost, your joy for written words and attention to detail was contagious. Mrs. Davis, you asked me to write a book in fourth grade about the Oregon Trail. I still have that book. You taught me to use my imagination. From that point forward, I wanted to become a writer.

To Dana Clark. Your small comment in college about becoming a communicator inspired me.

To Ed Ponton, Adam Hatton, Jim Musser, and Raborn Johnson. Thank you for challenging my assumptions in college. All four of you helped initiate my journey to figure out how faith and life mix.

To R&R Coffee Café and Waking Life. Thank you for inspiring me with excellent coffee!

To Chris Curran and Amy Lee. Thank you for reading early copies of this manuscript and helping me tell better stories.

To Bekah Warner, Bob Warner, Lindsey Eaton, Kim Callihan, Yongwon Lee, and Brianna Curran. Thank you for encouraging and supporting my family.

To my mentors Robert Brenner and Ken Schafer Jr. I don't know how to thank either one of you. Your encouragement and advice has been life changing. I love you both, very much!

Lastly, to Michael Erb, Emily Erb and Jarred Brackett. I can't put into words my love for each of you. Your unconditional love and support are the definition of true Christian community. I am humbled by your support of my family and me.

Notes

1. Visit 10dayswithout.com (see Partner Organizations).
2. "Children Out of Sight, Out of Mind, Out of Reach," UNICEF, last modified December 14, 2005, www.unicef.org/sowc06/press/release.php.
3. "Soles4Souls: What We Do," video, 2:26, Soles4Souls, http://soles4souls.org/our-mission.
4. "Soles4Souls," http://soles4souls.org/our-mission.
5. If you're brave enough to see what one of my feet looked like that day, check out this photo on my blog: http://danielryanday.com/warning-disturbing-image/.
6. "Soles4Souls," http://soles4souls.org/our-mission.
7. Visit 10dayswithout.com (see link for submitting your own story).
8. To see the video, go to www.youtube.com/watch?v=dIulK5UXfBY.
9. National Alliance to End Homelessness, *The State of Homelessness in America 2013* (April 2013), http://b.3cdn.net/naeh/bb34a7e4cd84ee985c_3vm6r7cjh.pdf.
10. This story has been told and retold by numerous people, and according to Wikipedia (http://en.wikipedia.org/wiki/The_Star_Thrower), the version most of us have heard is several variations removed from the original essay

written by Loren Eiseley. See Loren Eiseley, "The Star Thrower" in *The Unexpected Universe* (Orlando: Harcourt Brace, 1994), 67–92.

11. The Henry J. Kaiser Family Foundation, *Generation M² : Media in the Lives of 8- to 18-Year-Olds* (January 2010), http://kaiserfamilyfoundation.files.wordpress.com/2013/01/8010.pdf.

12. "The Desire for Desires," Social Issues Research Centre, www.sirc.org/articles/desire_for_desires.shtml, as cited in Doug Gross, "Have Smartphones Killed Boredom (and Is That Good)?," CNN, last modified September 26, 2012, www.cnn.com/2012/09/25/tech/mobile/oms-Smartphones-boredom/index.html?hpt=hp_c1.

13. Dr. Archibald D. Hart, *Thrilled to Death: How the Endless Pursuit of Pleasure Is Leaving Us Numb* (Nashville: Thomas Nelson, 2007), 11.

14. "Philip Zimbardo: The Demise of Guys?," video, 4:47, February 2011, TED, posted in August 2011, www.ted.com/talks/zimchallenge.html.

15. Kaiser, *Generation M²*, 42–45, http://kaiserfamily foundation.files.wordpress.com/2013/01/8010.pdf.

16. "A Tale of Two Cities," *Timothy Keller Podcast,* podcast audio, September 1, 2011, https://itunes.apple.com/us/podcast/timothy-keller-podcast/id352660924.

17. "Media and the End of Men," *The Phil Vischer Podcast,* podcast audio, November 27, 2012, https://itunes.apple.com/us/podcast/the-phil-vischer-podcast/id533006752.

18. "Poverty Overview," World Bank, www.worldbank.org /en/topic/poverty/overview.

19. Scott Todd, "The Church Will End Extreme Poverty," video, 11:53, Q, www.qideas.org/video/the-church-will -end-extreme-poverty.aspx.

20. "Water and Sanitation," One, www.one.org/c /international/issue/954/.

21. "World Facts and Statistics on Disabilities and Disability Issues," Disabled World, www.disabled-world.com /disability/statistics/.

22. See *Blue Letter Bible*, s.v. *"radah,"* www.blueletterbible.org /lang/lexicon/lexicon.cfm?strongs=H7287.

23. James Davison Hunter, *To Change the World: The Irony, Tragedy, and Possibility of Christianity in the Late Modern World* (New York: Oxford University Press, 2010), 174.

24. See www.ijmfreedommaker.org/campaign/501/10-Days -Without-Speech-/.

25. Statistics from: US Department of Health and Human Services, Children's Bureau, *Child Maltreatment 2011* (December 12, 2012), www.acf.hhs.gov/sites/default/files /cb/cm11.pdf; and US Government Accountability Office, *Child Maltreatment: Strengthening National Data on Child Fatalities Could Aid in Prevention* (July 2011), www.gao .gov/new.items/d11599.pdf.

About the Author

D aniel Ryan Day is a family man and storyteller. In 2005, he spent his summer in Romania working at a summer camp for orphans, which was a life-changing experience for him that began his desire to make a difference with his life. He's a proud graduate of Appalachian State University and Focus Leadership Institute. Daniel recently ran his first marathon and is now actively learning Spanish. (If you speak Spanish and run into him at an event, test him!) He loves berry bushes and grew up enjoying a small black-berry garden. (He would have had blueberry and raspberry bushes, but his dad kept running over them with the mower.) He is also a big fan of the Carolina Panthers and Atlanta Braves, even though their postseason records are embarrassing. Daniel loves to laugh and is known to quote Bill Cosby and Brian Regan regularly. He also loves fishing with his brother-in-law, even when he catches his ear instead of fish. (That happened only one time.) His biggest accomplishment is marrying his high school sweetheart in 2007. Daniel is currently the Director of Content for Axis, an organiza-tion that challenges students and families to move from apathy to compassionate social action. Meaning Axis offers deep content in a way that the next generation enjoys and understands. Daniel lives in Colorado with his wife, Rebecca, and their children: Noah, Finley, and Ava. This is Daniel's first book.

Hannah Lane Farmer/Hannah Lane Photography

Connect with Daniel:

Websites:

danielryanday.com

10dayswithout.com

Twitter:

@danielryanday

#10dayswithout

#intentionalchristian

Facebook:

Facebook.com/danielryanday

C.S. LEWIS
+
MTV

"Axis teams are more effective than any group I know in confronting students' apathy toward ideas." -- John Stonestreet, Breakpoint, Chuck Colson Center for Worldview, and Summit

The best way to describe Axis is like this: If you combined C.S. Lewis and MTV you would get Axis. Like Lewis, we pursue excellence in communication by synthesizing compelling ideas from books and lectures, and like MTV, we pursue excellence in production by curating art and media and presenting in a visually immersive way. We are culture translators. We exist to support and reinforce the incredible work that Churches and Christian Schools are doing in the lives of students and parents. Since 2007 we have led over 300 incredible spiritual emphasis weeks and multi-generational church events. Your audience will love the Axis content and style, they will be drawn closer to Jesus, and your mission will be honored and affirmed before students and parents by Axis. Everyone wins.

www.axis.org/info | booking@axis.org | 888-719-AXIS

Author photo by Michael Erb
follow him on Twitter: @journeyart

To inquire about having Daniel speak at your church, school, or event please email: booking@danielryanday.com or visit danielryanday.com/contact

Thank you for reading *Ten Days Without.* Seriously, it's a really big deal to me that you picked up this book and read it! I hope you were inspired, and that your inspiration leads to action on behalf of people in need. That's what *Ten Days Without* is about -- joining a movement to confront apathy by breaking down walls of indifference and being a voice for those who can't speak for themselves.

If you would like to take the ideas of *Ten Days Without* to the next level, I would love to work with your church, school, or event. My mission is to help people answer the question, "How can I live out my Christian faith so that it will significantly impact my family, career and community?"

Again, thank you for reading the book. I can't wait to become a part of what God is doing in your community.